P9-ELQ-825

ONE SMALL CANDLE

ONE
SMALL
CANDLE

*The Pilgrims' First Year In
America*

by
Thomas J. Fleming

 *New York*

W · W · NORTON & COMPANY · INC.

A portion of this book appeared in an article entitled "One Small Candle" in the December 1963 issue of *The Reader's Digest.*

Library of Congress Catalog Card No. 64-17513

Published simultaneously in the Dominion of Canada by George J. McLeod Limited, Toronto

PRINTED IN THE UNITED STATES OF AMERICA FOR THE PUBLISHERS BY THE VAIL-BALLOU PRESS, INC.
3 4 5 6 7 8 9

Contents

ONE SMALL CANDLE

Chapter 1

THE SWEET SHIP

The ship had never carried passengers. She was a
freighter, rather old and tired after more than fourteen years
of running taffeta and satins from Hamburg, hats and hemp
to Norway, wine and cognac from France. Thanks to the
wine, she was called a "sweet ship"—her hold full of pleasant
odors, in contrast to the foul fumes that rose from similar
ships of the day. Otherwise, riding high beside her dock at
Redriffe on the Thames, after discharging a cargo of wine
from Rochelle, France, on May 15, 1620, she was no different
from a hundred other square-riggers in this bustling section
of London Port.

Down the quay crowded with boxes and barrels and loung-
ing sailors came two men. One walked with a quick uneasy
gait, his eyes wary. The second was better dressed and carried himself with an expansive swagger. They stopped before
the ship, and the second man called out to a seaman repairing
sails on the sunny deck. "Ahoy, there. *Mayflower* of London?"

"Aye."

"Captain Christopher Jones?"

"Aye."

They were necessary questions. The old ship had a common name. Centuries later, confused historians would count at least twenty *Mayflowers* in the port records of the era. Two even fought on that historic day in 1588 when the seamen of Queen Elizabeth smashed Spain's mighty Armada and made the oceans of the world English territory.

Good Queen Bess was dead now, these seventeen years. Will Shakespeare, her reigning poet, was dead four years, although some of his plays—*Henry IV, Othello, Much Ado about Nothing*—still did a brisk business for the King's Men at Blackfriar's Theater. But the rest of England was neither prosperous nor content. An utterly different ruler now sat on the throne. Unstable, indecisive James I had done little since 1603 but drain the treasury with his extravagance, shock the nation with his morals, and embitter those who yearned for religious liberty.

Not that King James was any worse, or better, than his times. It was an age of excess. Elizabeth had had a fondness for extravagance, which once inspired the Earl of Hereford to greet her with three thousand footmen fitted out for the occasion with black and yellow feathers and gold chains. Under James, extravagance had become a passion. It was hard to tell London's fantastically dressed gallants from women. Ladies appeared at court in gowns that cost fifty pounds a yard for the embroidering alone. (In 1620 a pound was worth approximately fifty dollars.) The House of Cecil spent over fourteen hundred pounds hanging the bedroom of their Countess of Salisbury with white satin embroidered with gold, silver, and pearls to celebrate the birth of an heir. In a typical year, the king paid out five thousand pounds in "benevolences" to his favorites.

The manners and morals of the court were appalling. Banquets frequently turned into riots. A Venetian diplomat described one repast at St. James's Palace with its usual shoving, brawling crowd. "At the first assault, they upset the table and the crash of glass platters reminded me precisely of a severe hailstorm at midsummer smashing the window glass." When the lord mayor of London gave a dinner for the new Knights of Bath, the so-called gentlemen behaved outrageously with the citizens' wives. The sheriffs finally broke open a door and found Sir Edward Sackville in such a scandalous position that the entire banquet was forthwith abandoned.

Elsewhere the bucolic "merrie England" of song and story was rapidly vanishing. One justice of the peace wrote to a friend: "It is sessions with me every day all the day long here, and I have no time for my own occasions, hardly to put meat in my mouth. There was yesterday fourteen brought before me and presented that are so fit for no place as the House of Correction, all of one parish. . . ." Unemployment was widespread. "The number of poor do daily increase," one commentator wrote, "there has been no collection for them, no not these seven years, in many parishes of the land, especially in country towns: but many of those parishes turneth forth their poor, yea, and their lusty laborers that will not work, or for any misdemeanor want work, to beg, filch and steal for their maintenance . . . until the law bring them unto the fearful end of hanging." Men and women were regularly hanged for stealing as little as a loaf of bread. No one seemed to think twice about it, perhaps because a prison term was also tantamount to a death sentence, either from disease or the brutality of venal jailers.

It was an uneasy society, racked by vast changes in money, morals, and religion, with the last by far the greatest. Martin Luther's protest had sent a shock wave rolling through Europe. In country after country, rulers were struggling to control alarming new impulses toward personal freedom and spiritual independence. Perfectly logical, from a royal point of view. If a man was free to choose his religion one day, the next he might feel free to choose his king.

But the publication of the Bible in the vernacular had unleashed a power that no king could control—and no nation had taken to this new freedom more eagerly than England. "Theology rules here," said one visitor shortly after Elizabeth's death. The scandals of King James's court only convinced more and more people that England needed a deep infusion of Biblical religion if the nation was to survive. From secret printing presses in Scotland and Holland and Switzerland, Bible-inspired books and tracts poured into the country year after year, urging reform in the English Church as a first step to reforming a corrupt crown.

Others, despairing of reform, urged separation from the English Church and the right to join independent churches where men could worship as their consciences directed them. This was even more dangerous doctrine, and against these "Separatists" the royal fury was unchecked. Informers, sheriffs, constables, and bailiffs were under orders to "harry them out of the land."

Captain Christopher Jones of the *Mayflower* had no interest in such arguments. He was a solid, steady, respectable businessman of fifty with a wife and two children ashore and a one-fourth interest in his ship to guarantee his prosperity. Besides, he had spent most of his life at sea, more interested in reading charts and compasses than the Bible. Born in Harwich, the son of a prominent sea captain, he was hardly the sort of man to become involved with religious extremists. But the two men who greeted him in his comfortable "Great Cabin" on this lovely June day had a business proposition that was deeply involved with England's explosive religious dilemmas.

Robert Cushman was the name of the first man. He was mild mannered and nervous and described himself as a wool comber from Canterbury. The second man, bluff, hearty, full of jokes and good nature, did most of the talking. He was Thomas Weston, an ironmonger by trade but quick to make it clear that his money spoke for him in a dozen other businesses.

Weston was a born promoter and described in glowing terms the plans that he and some London friends had for starting a "plantation" in North America. Over seventy merchants and gentlemen were prepared to put up seven thousand pounds to launch a joint stock company for the venture. They would avoid all the mistakes that had turned Jamestown, Virginia, into a costly fiasco—yet to show a cent of profit after thirteen years of toil. Mr. Cushman was acting here as the representative of the prospective planters—sober, industrious Christians now sojourning in Holland because they disliked the king's religious conformity and wished to stay out of his majesty's jails. They had a royal patent for a tract of land on the American coast. All they needed was a ship. Would Captain Jones be interested?

Well. America was a long voyage, but ships were making it almost every month nowadays. What about money? Several years before, Jones had charged 160 pounds to a merchant who had chartered his ship for a voyage to Norway. On that trip Jones had proved himself a shrewd businessman, collecting his money even though his backer went into bankruptcy and charging thirty shillings for each day his ship was tied up in port during the litigation. The going rate for passengers on the Atlantic crossing in 1620 was about four pounds per person, and baggage went at three pounds a ton. Expenses during the passage ran to about three pounds a person when the shippers were responsible for supplying the food. But Weston and Cushman quickly reduced this charge by promising to bring their own provisions. Nonetheless, there was some hard bargaining in the *Mayflower's* Great Cabin before they settled on a figure. Jones insisted on a "demurrage" clause in their contract, entitling him to charge by the day if he was forced to linger on the American coast after he disembarked his passengers. Yielding this point, Weston and Cushman got Jones to agree on a price in the vicinity of four hundred pounds.

Good enough. But did Captain Jones want to go? A man his age, with a wife and family on shore, might well think twice about an Atlantic crossing.

For years Christopher Jones, like all his contemporaries, had been hearing and reading stories about America. The heroes of his Harwich youth were hometown men such as Christopher Newport, who had helped bring back the plunder from the fabulous Portuguese treasure ship *Madre de Dios* and, as admiral, had led the first expedition to Virginia in 1607. When Christopher Jones went to the theater, the stage was full of people like Captain Seagull in George Chapman's *Eastward Hoe!* with his wild tales of rubies and diamonds on the American seashore, or that weird native of the New World, Caliban, in William Shakespeare's last play, *The Tempest.* Almost every month saw a book by some captain or his more literate ship's surgeon describing new wonders and new coasts. It all made the life of a merchant sailor seem pretty tame. In his younger days Captain Jones had hunted whales off Greenland. Why not one more daring voyage, before old age crept up? The captain put out his hand. He was ready to take his ship across the vast, treacherous Atlantic.

Back at Henage House, a rabbit warren of tenements in the Aldgate section of London, Robert Cushman sat down to write a letter to his friends in Holland. If Christopher Jones could have seen it, he would almost certainly have had second thoughts about his agreement. Wearily Cushman lamented that "the many discouragements I find here . . . had made me to say I would give up my accounts to John Carver . . . and so leave it quite, with only the poor clothes on my back. But gathering up myself by further consideration, I resolved yet to make one trial more, and to acquaint Mr. Weston with the fainted state of our business." He went on to tell how Weston himself was equally discouraged, and "save for his promise, he would not meddle at all with the business any more; yet . . . at the last he gathered up himself a little more, and coming to me two hours after, he told me he would not yet leave it. And so advising together, we resolved to hire a ship. . . ."

Clearly, there was anything but harmony prevailing between the backers and the backed. But this was only one of the problems Weston and Cushman had neglected to mention to Christopher Jones. Far more alarming to a respectable businessman would have been the news that one of his passengers on the voyage would be a fugitive for whom King James had been ransacking Holland and England for over a year.

The man's name was William Brewster, and were it not for him, Robert Cushman would never have come to Christopher Jones in search of a ship. For eleven years Brewster had been the guiding spirit of the small band of exiles to which Cushman belonged. Trying to earn a living as a publisher, Brewster had made the mistake of printing a book attacking King James's plans to reorganize Scotland's Presbyterian Church along English lines. Copies were smuggled into Scotland and soon came to the king's attention.

His majesty flew into a royal rage and ordered his secretary of state to start an immediate manhunt for the printer. The trail led first to Holland and then back to London, where Brewster was assisting Cushman in the tortuous negotiations for a government grant of land in the New World. Brewster immediately went into hiding. He knew what would happen to him if the king's men caught him. For printing a similar book around the same time, a Scottish minister was fined three thousand pounds and sentenced to be whipped and set in the Pillory at Westminster, to have one of his ears cut off

and his nose slit, to be branded in the face with the letters
S.S. (Stirrer of Sedition), to be whipped and pilloried again
on a market day in Cheapside, to have the other ear cut off—
and be imprisoned for life. The king did not take religious
dissent lightly.

Cushman had written nervously to their friends in Holland: "Mr. B. is not well at this time: whether he will come
back to you or go into the north, I know not." When they
reported that bailiffs under the direction of the English ambassador to the Netherlands were scouring the country for
"one Brewster," the fugitive fled north, using the name Mr.
Williamson. At first Cushman continued the negotiations
alone, and then was joined by John Carver, a former London
merchant who had assisted him when these delicate dealings
with the king and the bishops first began, three long years
before.

Small wonder that Robert Cushman's nerves were taut.
Brewster's clash with the king had made his own situation
doubly precarious. As a Separatist, he was always liable to
arrest. The dickerings with the king, conducted through a
screen of sympathetic friends in high places, had been full of
alarming twists and turns. At first James had seemed to favor
the idea of letting dissenters go forth as colonists. He asked
how they would earn their living, and when he was told by
fishing, he exclaimed: "So God have my soul, 'tis an honest
trade! It was the Apostles' own calling!" But when it came
time for him to affix the Great Seal to a document guaran-
teeing the exiles' religious freedom in the New World, the
king suggested that the Separatists first have a conference
with the Archbishop of Canterbury. Since this would have

almost inevitably resulted in a prison sentence, the nego-
tiators wisely declined.

Even without the king's guarantee, they had continued to
negotiate with the Virginia Company, backers of Jamestown, for a "patent" giving them the right to found a "particular plantation" within their spacious domains. They had
persuaded one John Wincomb, a "religious gentleman" in the
household of the Countess of Lincoln, to play the part of a
respectable front man, and the Virginia Company had finally
issued a patent in his name. Ironically, Cushman and his
friends never made the slightest use of this document, on
which they had wasted three nerve-wracking years of negotiation. When they signed their agreement with Thomas
Weston, a new patent was promptly issued to John Pierce,
a London clothier and an associate of Weston's.

That had been in February. The future had had a victorious glow, then, after three dreary discouraging years. On the
same day, the Virginia Company had passed a very liberal
ordinance, giving captains and leaders of Particular Plantations "liberty till a form of government be here settled for
them, to associate unto themselves divers of the gravest and
discreetest of their companies to make orders, ordinances and
constitutions for the better ordering and directing of their
business, provided they be not repugnant to the laws of England." Freedom to make their own laws, to choose their own
leaders! For Cushman and his friends, who had suffered so
long from bad laws and worse rulers, it was almost unbe-
lievably good news.

But in the last three months, numerous complications had
arisen to make a "damp" in this original optimism. First there

was a sudden outburst of disagreement over their destination. Their patent permitted them to settle in "the northern part of Virginia," and they had decided on the mouth of "Hudson's River" as a likely place. But in 1614 Captain John Smith of Jamestown fame had done an excellent job of mapping the New World's coast from Maine to the tip of Cape Cod. He had named the area "New England" and come home to hymn its praises as the garden spot of the New World. Now a group of Englishmen, led by Sir Ferdinando Gorges, governor of the Port of Plymouth, were forming a separate company to colonize this coast. Weston and his friends heard about it and rushed to their would-be settlers urging them to plant there instead of on Hudson's River.

There was a possibility that the "Council for New England," as the new company was being called, would grant them a monopoly on the fishing rights. They could make a fortune. But the new company had yet to get a charter from the king, and this could take years. Moreover, in spite of John Smith's glowing description, other explorers had denounced New England as a land of intolerable snow and ice. One colony, led by Sir John Popham, had already expired after a disastrous winter in Maine. To the disgruntlement of their investors, the exiles announced that they preferred to stay within the boundaries of the Virginia Company.

Next came the problem of the "strangers." The original plans were to create a colony exclusively from the exiles in Holland. But volunteers turned out to be discouragingly few, and Weston had had to recruit several dozen people from London and the surrounding countryside. This was disturbing enough. But when it came to buying supplies, these newcomers demanded the right to have a representative on the purchasing committee.

Cushman and Carver, anxious to demonstrate their Christian charity, agreed. After all, these people were putting their money into the venture, too. But the representative, one Christopher Martin of Billerica, Essex, turned out to be a violent, headstrong personality who totally ignored his new confreres and rushed off to Kent, where he began buying up supplies at a fantastic rate, with no apparent attention to prices or planning. John Carver, fearful that Martin would spend every cent in the treasury with little to show for it, hurried down to Southhampton and began buying supplies too.

Weston and his fellow merchants were outraged. They wanted all the supplies bought in London, where they could save money through their business connections. Nor was this their last complaint. Weston had originally drawn up an agreement with the exiles in Holland, organizing a joint stock company to which he and his merchant friends would contribute money and the exiles labor for a period of seven years. During this time, all profits from "trade, traffic, trucking, working, fishing or any means" were to be credited to the joint account. At the end of that time, the profits were to be divided on the basis of the number of shares held by each person. The merchants bought shares at ten pounds each. The settlers were to earn a share for each person in their households over the age of sixteen.

Not the most generous terms in the world, but the breezy Weston had convinced the exiles that they could not do better elsewhere. Then he had found that most of the merchant backers were objecting violently to two clauses in the agreement. One stipulated that the settlers' houses would not be included in the final accounting of the company's net worth. The second gave the settlers the right to work two days a week for "the more comfort of themselves and their families." No, growled the hardnosed Londoners. That gave them too much incentive and time to work for themselves. Strike those two clauses, they told Weston, or we pull our money out of the whole venture.

Weston went to work on Robert Cushman with a potent mixture of threats and persuasion. Martin and Carver were both crying for more money. Carver alone said he needed some five hundred pounds. Between them, the two buyers had already spent the meager sums that the exiles in Holland had entrusted to the venture, and they had yet to hire a ship. As Cushman saw it, either he agreed to the changes or the whole project collapsed.

Cushman immediately found himself a target of recriminations from both sides. His friends in Holland accused him of making terms "fitter for thieves and bond slaves than honest men." Weston warned him that if his friends did not go along with his commitment, they could all "go scratch" for more money. "We will," Cushman moaned, "with going up and down, wrangling and expostulating, pass over the summer before we go. And to speak the truth, there is fallen already among us a flat schism: and we are readier to go to dispute than to set forward a voyage."

It was hardly a bright prospect that poor Cushman saw before him. He had invested every cent he had in the world in this colony, and had left wife and son behind in Holland during years of dangerous diplomacy. When he walked the streets of London, he found little to console him. All around him swirled the cruel vitality of the great city, the gallants with their "bombasted" or "beer barrel" breeches and gorgeous ruffs, the great ladies in their chaises with braces of footmen dashing before them to clear a path through the rabble, the tough pikemen of the town watch, ready and willing to break the head of any brawler, no matter how blue his blood.

Here came an exuberant flock of law students on their way to a new play by John Fletcher, whose gay comedies had replaced Elizabethan blood and thunder. There went a swirl of roaring young apprentices, fresh from the tavern, on the way to Paris Gardens across the Thames, where they would watch a Russian bear fight for his life against a swarm of mastiffs, or howl as an ape was dismembered by another pack of maddened dogs. Men and women staggered past, so drunk they could hardly see, bellowing bawdy verses. Drunkenness was so common in 1620 London that it was almost respectable. Ladies of the evening, wearing gowns cut low enough to make imagination superfluous, called invitingly from convenient doorways.

Exiled. Exiled. Even here in the heart of home. That was the real sorrow in Robert Cushman's heart as he walked the streets of London. Each year England seemed to drift further from the ideals he and his friends treasured. They could not know how many other men were thinking the same thoughts, and before the century was half over, those who revered the kingdom of God and those who revered the king of the realm would drench the nation in the bitter blood of civil war.

Robert Cushman and his friends would not have fought,

even if they had been offered the chance. They had already chosen the exile's path, and the path had lengthened slowly before their wondering eyes, until now it stretched from the green fields of England to a wilderness three thousand miles away. It was a deep and wonderful thing to them, this inward road they had traveled, which was now about to bring them and others to such a long voyage. It had echoes in it of Moses and the God who led the Chosen People into another wilderness. Robert Cushman and his friends had heard those echoes, and believed they were God's voice.

It was this deep fellowship in faith which sustained Robert Cushman and enabled him to accept criticisms and disappointments which would have disheartened many men. Even when the criticism came from his fellow church members, they were still his "brethen," and he took leave of them in his letters with "all love and affection."

In the next few days, contracts were signed and the *Mayflower* was officially hired. Cushman told Captain Jones that his friends were buying another ship in Holland which would accompany the *Mayflower* on the voyage and remain in the New World to reap (hopefully) fabulous profits in fishing and trading. They were to rendezvous in Southampton, England, in mid-July—little more than a month away.

That meant Captain Jones had no time to spare. He had to hire a crew—and for a long Atlantic voyage, men must be selected with care and forethought. For his first mate and pilot, Jones chose John Clark, who had made two previous voyages to America. It was a good choice on his record, and one that would prove even wiser in crises to come.

Jones knew little about the sea routes to America. It would be vital to have a man like Clark aboard, with his knowledge of currents and prevailing winds. Clark had made his first voyage to Virginia in 1610 as pilot under the strict and demanding Captain Sir Thomas Dale. That summer, the young sailor was captured by a Spanish caravel investigating Jamestown—a small but ominous reminder that there were other dangers on the ocean besides wind and waves. Taken to Madrid, Clark had been held prisoner for four years and intensively quizzed for his knowledge of sea routes to America.

Four years in a seventeenth-century prison would be enough to make most men swear off the sea for life. But in 1616, Clark was exchanged for a Spaniard held in London, and returned home to ship out promptly for Virginia again, this time with a load of cattle. No doubt about it, John Clark was a salt-water man, and Captain Christopher Jones must have rubbed his hands with satisfaction as his first mate signed his papers for the voyage.

Two more master's mates plus four quartermasters, a ship's carpenter, cooks, and gunners to man the *Mayflower's* ten cannon were soon on the rolls. Also a ship's doctor, one Giles Heale, licensed the year before by the honorable Company of Barber Surgeons. Young Heale came from the same parish as Thomas Weston—St. Giles in the Fields—and had been persuaded by that glib gentleman that there was profit and high adventure to be found aboard the good ship *Mayflower*.

Hiring the seamen was a lesser problem for Captain Jones. After a lifetime on deep water, he could size up a sailor at a glance. Not that he had an especially exquisite range of choices. Sailors of 1620 were fond of saying that "a man who went to sea for pleasure would be likely to go to hell for past-time." But with poverty and unemployment stalking the land, even the sailor's pittance of eighteen shillings a month looked good, and the *Mayflower's* complement of some thirty able seamen was soon full.

By now Christopher Jones had discovered that all was not sweetness and light between his passengers and their backers. It was not a good omen, this bickering. A ship's company needed harmony to survive on the high seas in 1620. Unhappy passengers could communicate their dissatisfactions to the crew, and in a week they could have a roaring mutiny on their hands. Jones knew from harsh experience how easily sailors could be incited to revolt. Only a few years before, a stranger had come aboard his ship while it was in port, led the crew in breaking into the wine, and started a riot which Jones and his mates had had to suppress with force.

But Christopher Jones had come to know Robert Cushman pretty well. He had learned how he and his friends had given up comfortable homes and jobs in England to live as common laborers in Holland because there they were part of a church that seemed to them the incarnation of the Christian spirit. This sounded a bit strong to Christopher Jones, who had heard more blasphemy than prayers from his congregations at sea. Like most men of action he was a skeptic at heart. But he had traveled around the world enough to be surprised at nothing. He would judge these people as he judged everyone else—face to face, on their deeds and not on their words. If there was anything extraordinary about these exiles, they would have to prove it to the captain of the *Mayflower*.

Chapter 2

ANSWERABLE COURAGES

While Christopher Jones was hiring his crew and overhauling his ship for the long voyage, his prospective passengers were equally busy in Holland. But while Jones proceeded with the practiced calm of the experienced professional, his passengers made their preparations for the journey with uneasy, mournful hearts. Many were by no means certain that they should exchange the peace and prosperity of Holland for the dubious prospects of an unmapped wilderness.

They had spent eleven years in Leyden, bustling center of Holland's world famed cloth industry. Life had not been easy for them. Country people, used to living off the land, they had had to toil as weavers and spinners in the city's cloth factories. Others became serge workers, twine makers, hatters, goldsmiths. The hours were long and the pay modest, but the majority managed to make an acceptable living, and a few of the more gifted and industrious, such as thirty-year-old William Bradford, became almost comfortable.

Like many other members of the little church, Bradford had begun his adult life in Leyden. In 1613 he had married Dorothy May, the daughter of a prominent, well-to-do English family from Amsterdam, bought his own home, and become a citizen. All this took sacrifice. Six days a week Bradford worked twelve and fourteen hours weaving fustian, an expensive twilled cloth made from cotton and linen. He had little time to give to his only son John. His young wife, only sixteen when they married, was lonely for her friends and family in Amsterdam, and doted on the five-year-old boy to the point where he was in danger of being badly spoiled.

William Bradford was used to sacrifices. He had begun making them early in his life. Orphaned in boyhood, he had spent a sickly, unhappy childhood among complaining relatives. While still in his early teens, he had walked from his native Austerfield across the fields to Scrooby and met William Brewster, bailiff of the manor and keeper of the King's Post on the Great North Road. At that time Brewster, in his mid-forties, was a man of local wealth and importance. In his youth he had studied at Cambridge and served as trusted assistant to Queen Elizabeth's secretary of state. He had returned to his native countryside when his adventures in the world of kings and courtiers were abruptly ended by his patron's fall from royal favor.

Between the genial man of the world and the lonely uncertain country youth, there had flamed something unique: a recognition of spiritual kinship that was to endure until death. Brewster gave Bradford books to read, and talked freely to him about his religious beliefs. Already he had gathered around him a small group of thoughtful men and women who felt the need of a purer, more personal religion.

Soon, to the horror of his relatives, William Bradford was attending the secret meetings of the little "church" at Scrooby Manor. Bradford's father had been a yeoman— among the principal landholders of Austerfield. But for Bradford, the bailiff of Scrooby Manor was father, teacher, and priest, and when the spies and informers of the local bishop began hounding those who met at Scrooby, Bradford sold his lands and followed Brewster into exile.

William Bradford never uttered a word of regret for this decision. From his early teens, he was a man who knew his own mind with remarkable sureness. In Leyden, he says, they found "peace and spiritual comfort," which they valued "above any other riches." No spies or informers molested them. They worshipped each Sunday in the spacious house that William Brewster had bought for their pastor in Bell Alley, not far from the vast fourteenth-century basilica of St. Peter.

They modeled their church and their lives on the example of the first Christians. Robert Cushman and John Carver were deacons. William Brewster was the ruling elder. All were united under the solemn vow or "covenant" which bound them to share their love and prayers and if necessary their money and property. Edward Winslow, a young printer from Droitwich, England, who joined the church not long after it was formed, later said: "I persuade myself never people on earth lived more lovingly together . . . than we the Church at Leyden did."

Thanks largely to Brewster, they had found an extraordinary pastor. John Robinson was a Cambridge graduate who had been ordained a priest of the Church of England. But like many other men, he had gradually become convinced from studying the Bible that for him, at least, this was not the right path to genuine religion. He came to this decision with regret. Instead of castigating bishops and canons, the way many other reformers did, Robinson wrote: "I esteem so many in that Church, . . . for my Christian brethren, and myself a fellow member with them of that one mystical body of Christ scattered far and wide throughout the world that I have always, in spirit and affection, all Christian fellowship and communion with them." In contrast to the quarrels that tore several of the reformed churches in Amsterdam and made them the laughingstock of England, the Church of Leyden was a model of peace and harmony under Robinson's gentle guidance.

Why were they leaving such a pastor and this beautiful city, famous for its lovely waterways, sunlit squares, and scrupulously neat streets? There were many reasons. New war was looming between Holland and Spain. In 1574, during the first war of liberation, Leyden had withstood a savage siege in which half its 100,000 citizens had died of starvation or disease. The Dutch, eager to have England as an ally, might be forced to placate King James and suppress this refugee church whose ruling elder had published a seditious book. The long arm of the English king had already been demonstrated when his ambassador sent Dutch bailiffs searching through Leyden for William Brewster.

There was also the exile's yearning to stand upon a piece of soil and say: "This is mine." The leaders of the church had been men of property in England. But land was not by any means their overriding motive. Far more important was their concern for the future of their children.

"Many . . . that were of best dispositions and gracious inclinations," William Bradford says, "having learned to bear the yoke in their youth and willing to bear part of their parents' burden, were oftentimes so oppressed with their heavy labours that though their minds were free and willing, yet their bodies bowed under the weight of the same, and became decrepit in their early youth, the vigour of nature being consumed in the bud as it were." Many other young people refused to bear the burden. They threw the "reins from their necks" and, departing from their parents, "some became soldiers, others took upon them far voyages by sea, and others some worse courses."

It was inevitable that some of the younger exiles would be attracted by the high-spirited traditions of Holland. The Dutch youth of 1620 were extremely emancipated. One English visitor noted: "The women of these parts give great liberty to their daughters. Sometimes by chance they slide on the ice till the gates of the city be locked, and the young men feast them at Inns in the suburbs all the night, or till they please to take rest. . . . Sometimes the young men and virgins agree . . . to be drawn with horses upon sledges to cities 10–20 or more miles distant and there feast all night, and this they do without all suspicion of unchastity, the hostesses being careful to lodge and oversee the women."

The exiles could visualize their children disappearing into this wealthy, easy-living society, forgetting that they were

English, much less people with a special call from God. "They saw," Bradford says, "their posterity would be in danger to degenerate and be corrupted." So, as early as 1617, they had begun to debate the wisdom of finding another refuge. Three years of hesitation and negotiation, of pondering such books as Sir Walter Raleigh's *Discoverie of Guiana,* had followed. Raleigh had praised Guiana as a region of perpetual spring, virgin soil, and abundant gold mines. But the proximity of the Spaniards discouraged the Leyden exiles. Fifty years before, French Protestants had tried to settle in Florida. Some four hundred were slaughtered by Spanish raiders, for the simple crime of trespassing on dominions that the Pope had given to the king of Spain.

The northern coasts of America seemed more promising. But here, too, there were problems. Everyone by now knew the shocking mortality that had all but destroyed the settlement at Jamestown. Nine out of every ten settlers had died within a year. Of the twelve hundred who had gone out in 1619, a thousand had died by 1620. Prophets of doom in the congregation predicted that the same thing would happen to them.

"The length of the voyage was such as the weak bodies of women and other persons worn out with age and travail (as many of them were) could never be able to endure," is how William Bradford recalls their warnings. If they survived the voyage, there were the "miseries of the land"—famine, nakedness, the change of diet and air to "infect their bodies with sore sicknesses and grievous diseases."

If they survived these horrors, there were the savages to worry about, "cruel, barbarous and most treacherous, being

most furious in their rage and merciless where they overcome; not being content only to kill and take away life, but
delight to torment men in the most bloody manner that may
be; flaying some alive with the shells of fishes, cutting off
the members and joints of others by piecemeal and broiling
on the coals, [they] eat the collops of their flesh in their
sight whilst they live."

Finally there was the problem of money. A fortune had
been spent to settle Virginia. Where would they get money
to "fit them with necessaries," not to mention the expense of
shipping? Moreover, "many precedents of ill success and
lamentable miseries befallen others in the like designs were
easy to be found, and not forgotten to be alleged." Probably
the example that made the deepest impression on the exiles
was the fate of 180 fellow Separatists who had left Amsterdam in 1618 under the leadership of Francis Blackwell.
They had been arrested in England, and Blackwell had denied his Separatist principles under oath, betraying a number of fellow believers in order to escape the clutches of the
bishops. But the ship in which his 180 disciples were
"packed like herrings" had been driven far off its course by
storms, the water had run low, and disease had broken out
killing the captain, Blackwell, and many of the crew. Only
fifty starved skeletons had staggered ashore at Jamestown,
where, no doubt, more than half of these soon expired.

"The very hearing of these things could not but move the
very bowels of men to grate within them and make the weak
to quake and tremble," William Bradford admits. But "some
of the cheefest thought otherwise." Bradford's modesty does
not permit him to name these "cheefest." But he was one of

them. There was something about this young yeoman that made him a natural leader.

Thus in Bradford's memorable words, the prophets of doom were told that "all great and honourable actions are accompanied with great difficulties and must be both enterprised and overcome with answerable courages." No one denied the dangers; they were "great, but not desperate." The difficulties were many "but not invincible." It was true that such attempts were not to be made "without good ground and reason, not rashly or lightly as many have done for curiosity or hope of gain." But "their ends were good and honourable, their calling lawful and urgent; and therefore they might expect the blessing of God in their proceeding."

They had taken a vote at the end of this debate, and a majority of the congregation decided to stay in Holland. This meant that Pastor Robinson would have to stay with them. But the "cheefest" were still determined to move, and they decided to send their youngest and best men as advance guards to found a plantation. If they were successful, Robinson and the others vowed they would join them as quickly as possible. For their spiritual leadership, they would rely on Elder William Brewster until Robinson rejoined them.

So they had begun their voyage, and had sent William Brewster, John Carver, and Robert Cushman to England to "put this design in execution." Years of frustrating delay and negotiation followed. The king would not grant them true freedom, the Virginia Company was glad to have them as colonists but was too bankrupt to supply them with shipping, and the Dutch offered to back them in a colony at the mouth of Hudson's River but would not promise to defend them if the English, French, or Spanish attacked. Finally, in February, 1620, Thomas Weston appeared in Leyden with his offer from the London merchants.

Weston obviously saw these exiles as plums for picking. He treated them with the artful condescension a man of the world displays to country bumpkins. When they decided to buy a ship in Holland to transport themselves to England, and for use in the New World, he ragged them unmercifully over their choice of a 60-ton vessel which they rechristened the *Speedwell*. Looking for a bargain, the exiles bought cheap and then found that the vessel needed extensive repairs, including new masts.

"Mr. Weston makes himself merry with our endeavours about buying a ship," Pastor Robinson wrote ruefully to John Carver in England. By this time (June 4, 1620) they had learned about the changes in the terms of agreement. Mr. Weston was not only a merry gentleman but a tricky one. It was intolerable to ask men "to serve a new apprenticeship of seven years, and not a day's freedom from tasks." This had discouraged a number of volunteers who had withdrawn from the enterprise. As for William Bradford and others who had money in the general fund, they, too, were so discouraged that not a man "would pay anything if he had again his money in his purse."

By now there were only twenty-seven people willing to go. An attempt had been made to recruit volunteers among the Separatists in Amsterdam, but the democratic ways of the Church of Leyden were "ratts bane" to these stern Christians, and they soon demanded their money back.

More and more the venture seemed to be tinged with imminent disaster. But men like William Bradford meant what they had said about "answerable courages." They had sold their houses and furniture and given up their jobs. It was either sail or starve.

Yet Bradford betrayed his own doubts about the voyage by refusing to take his son John with him. Many others took their children. Issac Allerton, the tailor, brought his pregnant wife Mary and three small children. William White, the wool comber, took his pregnant wife Susanna and five-year-old son Resolved. Mary Brewster, the fugitive's wife, brought her two youngest children, but left behind her two older daughters with her son Jonathan, age twenty-seven. Others followed Mrs. Brewster's example and split their families. Francis Cooke and Thomas Rogers each brought along a son but no wife. A few left both wives and children behind—Doctor Samuel Fuller, Blacksmith Moses Fletcher.

These sixteen men, eleven women, and their nineteen children—less than a sixth of the Church of Leyden—were hardly the warrior band one might recruit to challenge a wilderness. The first settlers in Virginia had all been men. Almost every other colony had followed a similar policy. Never before had any English expedition attempted the New World with so many families and children.

Now it was time to declare "a day of solemn humiliation" to seek God's guidance and blessing. They all came together at their pastor's house in Bell Alley and heard Robinson preach on a text from Ezra, 8.21. *And there at the River, at Ahava, I proclaimed a fast that we might humble ourselves before our God and seek of him a right way for us, and for our children and for all our substance.*

Edward Winslow never forgot the advice Robinson gave them. "He charged us before God and His blessed angels to follow him no further than he followed Christ. And if God should reveal anything to us by any other instrument of His, to be as ready to receive it as ever we were to receive any truth by his ministry. For he was very confident the Lord had more truth and light yet to break forth out of His holy Word. . . . But withal exhorted us to take heed what we received for truth, and well to examine and compare and weigh it with other scriptures of truth before we receive it; for saith he, it is not possible that the Christian world should come so lately out of such thick anti-Christian darkness, and that full perfection of knowledge should break forth at once."

After the sermon, Winslow tells us, "they that stayed at Leyden feasted us that were to go. . . . We refreshed our selves, after our tears, with singing of Psalms, making joyful melody in our hearts as well as with the voice, there being many of the Congregation very expert in music; and indeed it was the sweetest melody that ever mine ears heard."

The next morning almost the entire congregation went with the voyagers to Delftshaven, a port some twenty-four miles from Leyden, where the *Speedwell* was waiting for them. They boarded the roomy canal boats at Nuns Bridge, near the pastor's house at Green Gate. In a few minutes they were gliding down the Vliet, as the section of the canal between Leyden and Delftshaven is still called. Through the huge water gate in the city's massive walls they sailed and then past the lush farms and pasture lands of the Dutch countryside.

As Leyden receded into the distance, more than one of the voyagers turned for a last look at its lofty roofs and spires, thinking wistfully of the peaceful, happy years they had spent there. Many, such as William Bradford and Edward Winslow who had begun their married lives there, were flooded by tender memories. The pangs of their parting still live in William Bradford's words: "And so they left that good and pleasant city, which had been their resting place near twelve years; but they knew they were pilgrims, and looked not much on these things, but lifted up their eyes to the heavens, their dearest country, and quieted their spirits."

Nine miles from Leyden, the canal made a sharp turn to the left and flowed beneath the Hoorn Bridge. Now they sailed quietly beside the main road from the Hague to Delft, lined with tall ancient trees. Through the heart of Delft, then famous throughout Europe for its pottery, they went, passing the Old Kirk with its lancet windows and graceful leaning tower. Soon they were on the canal called the Schie, and finally into that miracle of Dutch engineering the Delftshaven Canal, which flowed toward the sea between miles of dikes high above the surrounding pasture land. Next came sets of sluice gates that gently lifted their barge into the harbor, and across the quiet sunlit water to the side of the *Speedwell*.

Bradford, Pastor Robinson, and a few others went aboard and conferred with Captain Reynolds and the English crew who had been sent from London to take over the ship. They had all signed up to serve the colony for a full year in the

New World. Also aboard was a pilot, Robert Coppin, who had recently returned from a voyage to Virginia. Here was living proof that a man could survive the terrors of the Atlantic.

To skeptical eyes, the 60-ton *Speedwell* seemed hardly a match for the mighty ocean. She was a "pinnace," a sailing craft smaller than a typical cargo ship, probably not much more than forty feet long. But the passengers were somewhat reassured by recalling that the *Godspeed,* one of the ships on the maiden voyage to Jamestown, had been a mere forty tons and another, the *Discovery,* only twenty tons.

Soon down the quay came a smiling crowd, some of them friends from Leyden who had traveled by road to see them off, others friends from the English church in Amsterdam. Dorothy Bradford's father was an elder of the Amsterdam church, and since the Leyden exiles had spent almost a year in Amsterdam when they first came to Holland, there were many other ties. The well-wishers escorted the departing ones into the town, and another brotherly feast was spread for them. "That night was spent with little sleep by most," William Bradford says, "but with friendly entertainment and Christian discourse and other real expressions of true Christian love."

The next day the wind was fair, and the *Speedwell's* captain said he was ready to sail. Down to the dock they went once more, and there the Bradfords made their heartbreaking farewell with their only son John. Other equally painful goodbyes were said.

Edward Winslow tells us that many "were not able to speak one to another for the abundance of sorrow to part."

How deeply the Bradfords felt the farewell can be seen in the father's own words: "Truely doleful was the sight of that sad and mournful parting: to see what sighs and sobs and prayers did sound amongst them, what tears did gush from every eye, and pithy speeches pierced each heart; that sundry of the Dutch strangers that stood on the quay as spectators could not refrain from tears. . . . But the tide (which stays for no man) calling them away that were thus loath to depart, their reverend pastor falling down on his knees (and they all with him) with watery cheeks commended them with most fervent prayers to the Lord and his blessing."

As the *Speedwell* eased away from the dock, Captain Reynolds, perhaps with a thought to cheering his mournful passengers, had his sailors fire a farewell volley from their muskets, to which his gunners replied with booms from three of the ship's cannon. Such fireworks were small consolation to the saddened voyagers. But they did give the departure the aura of an historic occasion.

Chapter 3

THE STRANGERS

Out across the calm July waters of the English Channel sailed the little *Speedwell*, heading west to Southampton. This rendezvous had been chosen to avoid interference from either the bishops or the king. The exiles remembered what had happened to Francis Blackwell and his ill-fated congregation when they attempted to sail from London. There was not much support for the king's religious policy in the west of England. Besides, if all went well, they would not be in port for more than a day.

As the wind rose and the *Speedwell* began heaving through the Channel's mild swells, exclamations of alarm came from Captain Reynolds. He did not like the way the ship was handling. He was heard to mutter that only a fool would have put such masts and sails on a 60-ton pinnace. With every swell, water poured over the decks and cascaded down on the hapless passengers below as if the seemingly solid planks were nothing more than sieves. It was a "wet ship." In the language of the day, this meant that age and the pounding of the seas had "worked" the planks of the deck until they had separated so far that no amount of caulking could keep the water out.

This was common in sailing ships. It made for discomfort, but it was hardly a serious problem. So it was with excited happiness the voyagers crowded the rails to see the lofty chalk cliffs of Dover, their first glimpse of home in twelve years. Past Eastbourne, Worthing, Brighton, and Portsmouth they sailed, and finally, past the Isle of Wight into Southampton water. There, tied up at the West Quay, was the brown and gold *Mayflower*. She had sailed from London over a week before, and had been waiting for them for seven days.

Staying carefully belowdeck was "Mr. Williamson," better known to the Leyden travelers as their beloved elder William Brewster. He had crept aboard the ship at Southampton, still heavily disguised, and he was not to show his head abovedeck until they were well at sea. For William Bradford, seeing his old friend and mentor again after almost two years was a joyous occasion, and his personal pleasure was shared by all. Equally pleasant were the reunions with Robert Cushman and John Carver, who greeted their families and friends after long separations.

But Cushman, Carver, and Mr. Williamson were by no means alone. Aboard the *Mayflower*, along with Captain Jones and his crew, were some eighty "strangers" who had sailed from London. These were the volunteers whom Thomas Weston and his business friends had recruited in London and its vicinity to fill out the plantation's quota.

Some, like Christopher Martin, were dissatisfied with the Church of England and quite ready to join the kind of church the Leyden exiles had created. Others had obviously succumbed to the Weston vision of profits in the wilderness and, like millions who came after them, were heading for the New World to make their fortunes. Stephen Hopkins was almost certainly one of these. He had already made one voyage to Virginia, and had survived a harrowing shipwreck in Bermuda. Now he was sailing on the *Mayflower* with his pregnant wife Elizabeth and their three children. He was a man of considerable means and had brought along two servants, Edward Dotey and Edward Leister, both of London. Another of the "strangers" was John Billington, a surly, contentious character with a viper-tongued wife and two unruly teen-age sons. More devout was well-to-do William Mullins, boot and shoe dealer of Dorking. He was bringing his wife and two children, Joseph and Priscilla. Mullins had bought nine shares in Weston's company— equal to an investment of about one hundred pounds—and he had a large supply of shoes in the ship's hold, no doubt the last of his stock.

Also on board were a number of servants hired by either Jones or Cushman for the Leyden group. Husky twenty-eight-year-old John Howland was to do the heavy labor in the wilderness for Deacon Carver. Twenty-two-year-old William Butten was to do likewise for Doctor Samuel Fuller. Eleven men, one woman, and six children were on this helper's list. The children were all orphans, probably illegitimate. There were thousands of them roaming the streets of 1620 London, and the city fathers had taken to rounding them up and shipping them in lots of one hundred to Virginia. There anyone who would pay three pounds for their fare and two pounds for their clothing could acquire them as servants. Like the apprentices of 1620, these servants were "bound" or indentured under a strict contract, which stipulated that they had to work from four to seven years without pay to settle the debt of transporting them. With the wrong master, this arrangement could turn out to be little more than slavery; it rarely made for happy, contented workers.

Equally important to the venture were two "master mariners"—Thomas English and John Allerton—and two ordinary seamen who were to man the 10-ton sloop or "shallop" stored between decks on the *Mayflower*. They were under contract to stay in the New World for a year, like Captain Reynolds and his crew aboard the *Speedwell*. The shallop would be essential for exploring the shallow waters along the coast.

One other hired man of considerable importance was redheaded Captain Miles Standish, a short, stocky, tough ex-soldier who had been signed to handle the plantation's defenses. Now a man of about thirty-four, Standish had served with the English army sent by Queen Elizabeth to aid Holland against Spain. The last English troops had been withdrawn from Holland in 1609, about the time that the first of the Scrooby exiles were making their way to Amsterdam and finally Leyden. It is possible that Standish first met them in Holland, and when the time came, they remembered this pugnacious warrior as the right man to superintend their military affairs. For Standish, whose only trade was soldiering, it was a welcome offer; between wars, the English government had an unpleasant habit of discharging its best men, leaving them either to steal or starve. Childless, the captain brought along only his wife Rose.

This, then, was the mixed company that greeted the Leyden exiles as the *Speedwell* tied up beside the *Mayflower* at Southampton's West Quay. The pleasure of seeing William Brewster, John Carver, and Robert Cushman soon vanished when they realized that these "strangers," if their servants were counted, actually outnumbered them—and if their spokesman, Christopher Martin, was typical of their attitude, the plantation could look forward to nothing but acrimony and chaos. Between them, Martin and Carver had spent over seven hundred pounds on provisions, with Martin accounting for the lion's share. But when they asked him for a coherent statement of his expenditures, he flew into a fantastic rage and refused. "If he be called upon for accounts," Robert Cushman wrote a London friend, "he crieth out of unthankfulness for his pains and care, that we are suspicious of him: and flings away and will end nothing."

Cushman had good reason to dislike Martin. The brusque Essex man had singled him out for special excoriation for conceding the changes in the articles of agreement. "He said he never received no money on those *conditions,*" Cushman raged to his friend. "He was not beholden to the Merchants for a pin! They were bloodsuckers! and I know not what. Simple man! He indeed never made any Conditions with the Merchants, nor ever spake with them. But did all that money fly to Southampton, or was it his own? Who will go and lay out money so rashly and lavishly as he did and never know how he comes by it, or on what conditions?"

Unfortunately, poor Cushman found no support among his brethren from Leyden. They were as unhappy with him as they were with Martin. Cushman protested that he had notified John Carver of the changes and had received his approval. But Carver denied it, saying he was so busy buying supplies he had left all negotiations to his fellow deacon.

In the midst of these hot words, who should appear from London but their old friend Thomas Weston himself, with the revised articles of agreement for all to sign. He got a flat no from everybody. They were not going to become bond servants for seven years. They were still perfectly willing to fulfill the agreement in the original articles—but their houses and those two precious days a week of free labor they insisted on having for themselves. This threw Weston into a rage which made Martin's temper seem mild. In a complete huff he went back to London, telling them contemptuously they would now have to "stand on their own legs."

The ironmonger refused to advance them another cent, not even enough to pay the sixty pounds they still owed to various merchants for ordered supplies. This meant they would have to sell some of the food already purchased in order to clear the port.

From his poop deck, Captain Jones watched all this wrangling with growing apprehension. After seven days in port, the crew was growing restless. Many of the passengers, seeing the dissension among the leaders, were talking about going home.

By now the hold of the *Mayflower* was crammed with the tons of supplies needed for passengers and crew. Barrels of salt beef and cod and sacks of smoked beef, huge barrels of beer and water, tubs of pickled eggs, barrels of biscuits, boxes of smoked herring had been lugged and hoisted and rolled aboard during the seven-day wait.

With the supplies had come another hired hand, a twenty-one-year-old cooper named John Alden. By royal command, every ship clearing an English port had to have a cooper aboard to watch over the precious barrels of beer and water, sample them, and if necessary tighten them to make sure air was not getting in to spoil the contents. If the ship discharged some of its barrels, it was up to the cooper to hammer together an equal number for the return trip, so England would not be shortchanged in precious wood. The husky, blond young Alden had been hired for a year with the understanding that he could leave the plantation at the end of his contract, or stay as a settler if he chose.

Now, the passengers had to confer with Alden and Captain Jones to decide which of their provisions they could most easily spare. Jones recommended the butter, which they had apparently overbought. So they sold "four score firkins," about four thousand pounds, and paid their debts. Then they sat down and wrote a pleading letter to Weston and his associates in London. It began with a long and involved explanation of why they could not accept the amended articles of agreement which Robert Cushman had had no authority to sign. Then came an honest attempt to make a settlement:

"Since you conceive yourselves wronged as well as we, we

thought meet to add a branch to the end of our ninth article as will almost heal that wound of itself, which you conceive to be in it. But that it may appear to all men that we
are not lovers of ourselves only, but desire also the good
and enriching of our friends who have adventured your
moneys with our persons, we have added our last article to
the rest, promising you again by letters in the behalf of the
whole company that if large profits should not arise within
the seven years, that we will continue together longer with
you if the Lord give a blessing. This we hope is sufficient to
satisfy any in this case, especially friends."

Having offered to extend the share-the-wealth agreement
almost indefinitely, the voyagers obviously felt that generosity could do no more. So they turned to the serious short-
ages which only the merchants and their cash could solve.

"We are in such a strait at present, as we are forced to sell
away sixty pounds worth of our provisions to clear the
haven, and withal to put ourselves upon great extremities,
scarce having any butter, no oil, not a sole to mend a shoe,
nor every man a sword to his side, wanting many muskets,
much armour, etc. And yet we are willing to expose ourselves to such eminent dangers as are like to ensue, and trust
to the good providence of God, rather than His name and
truth should be evil spoken of, for us. Thus saluting all of
you in love and beseeching the Lord to give a blessing to
our endeavour, and keep all our hearts in the bonds of peace
and love, we take leave and rest."

This rather forlorn attempt to reconcile the London busi-
nessmen before sailing away into the unknown was absolutely necessary from the voyagers' point of view, because

no one in the group had any illusion that the plantation would become self-sufficient immediately. As in Virginia, they planned to rely on ships from home for food and clothing, and make their profits from fishing and trading for furs with the Indians. If Weston really meant what he said about leaving them to stand on their own legs, they were sailing to almost certain doom.

Fortunately, at this crucial moment they were heartened by a letter from their pastor, John Robinson. Obviously unhappy that he was not going with them ("How willingly . . . I would have borne my part with you in this first brunt, were I not from strong necessity held back"), Robinson urged them to place their total trust in God and try to practice perfect Christian charity toward each other. He urged them neither to give nor take offense especially toward those who were strangers among them. He devoted another earnest exhortation to the need for everyone to work for the common good. Finally came his most significant words: "Whereas you are to become a body politic, using amongst yourselves civil government, and are not furnished with any persons of special eminency above the rest to be chosen by you into office of government, let your wisdom and godliness appear, not only in choosing such persons as do entirely love and will promote the common good, but also yielding unto them all due honour and obedience in their lawful administrations. . . . "

The letter was read to the assembled company on the deck of the *Speedwell*. It takes an effort of imagination for us, its inheritors, to realize how unusual these words were. They were being read to people a few feet away from a shore where the king's power was almost absolute, and those who lacked noble blood in their veins had no hope, much less the possibility, of ruling other men. For a thousand years, men of "special eminency" had ruled in Europe, and were ruling in the colonies of Spain, Portugal, Holland. Even in Virginia their rule still prevailed, simply because it was, to men of 1620, the way things were done. But these voyagers had found in their exile a different way, rooted in a new sense of individual worth and a new kind of solidarity.

Warmed by their pastor's words, they made final preparations for the trip. The passengers were divided, about eighty to the *Mayflower* and thirty to the *Speedwell*. Most of the leaders preferred the roomier *Mayflower*, but Captain Reynolds protested that he wanted some prominent names on the *Speedwell* to keep order among his passengers and make sure his little ship would not be left in the lurch if a crisis came. William Bradford volunteered along with several others. "The chief of them that came from Leyden," he says, "went in this ship to give the master content." Finally, "governors" were appointed for each ship. Christopher Martin drew the assignment for the *Mayflower*, with Robert Cushman for his assistant. These men would have absolute authority, while on shipboard, to settle all disputes arising between passengers.

They were now as ready as they would ever be, and they informed Captain Reynolds and Captain Jones that they could sail with the first fair wind.

Their minds heavy with their internal dissensions and worry about the apparent desertion of their vitally needed backers, the voyagers had no doubt forgotten all about the difficulties of the *Speedwell*. But Reynolds and Jones had spent the days consumed by their passenger's wrangles going over the *Speedwell* with Southampton shipwrights, who had suggested several changes in her sails and rigging. For the two captains, the question was simple but potentially huge: if the *Speedwell* handled badly in the mild seas of the Channel, how would she fare on the heaving Atlantic? There was only one way to find out.

Chapter 4

GOD'S CHOSEN PEOPLE?

Down the Solent, that narrow body of water between the Isle of Wight and England, and into the Channel went the *Mayflower* and the *Speedwell*. It was August 5, already late in the year for a voyage to the New World. It would have been far better to have left in the late spring, when the Atlantic winds were more favorable, and have arrived in time to build houses and explore the country in mild summer weather. They had already lost two precious months in argument and hesitation. Even so, with a good crossing they could still arrive by early October, and have some kind of shelter before the worst of winter came.

But not even this mild share of good fortune was to be theirs. First they ran into unfavorable winds, which left them beating about the Channel for several days, unable to make any real headway. Then Captain Reynolds of the *Speedwell* began raising and lowering one of his sails—the signal of distress. Both ships came about, and Reynolds put off from the *Speedwell* in a small boat for a conference with Captain Jones.

Reynolds had grim news. The *Speedwell* was leaking badly. He had to keep men working the pumps continuously, and still the water was rising steadily in the hold. To attempt an ocean crossing in such condition was out of the question. There was only one thing to do—get her into a dry dock. Jones suggested Dartmouth, a few miles down the coast from Southampton. Reynolds agreed, and by the next day the *Speedwell* was being examined by another team of local shipwrights.

It was disheartening and demoralizing, especially for those who had not exactly enjoyed their first few days at sea. Among the outstanding problems was seasickness and the outrageous behavior of Christopher Martin. Robert Cushman was undone by both. In a mournful letter to his friend in London, he declared they would never meet again in this world because "an infirmity of body has seized me, which will not in all likelihood leave me till death. What to call it I know not, but it is a bundle of lead, as it were, crushing my heart more and more these fourteen days; as that although I do the actions of a living man, yet I am but as dead, but the will of God be done."

As for the expedition, Cushman could not have been more discouraged. "Our pinnace will not cease leaking, else I think we had been halfway to Virginia. Our voyage hither hath been as full of crosses as ourselves have been of crookedness. We put in here to trim her; and I think as others also, if we had stayed at sea three or four hours more, she would have sunk right down. And though she was twice trimmed at Hampton, yet now she is as open and leaky as a sieve; and there was a board a man might have pulled off with his fingers, two foot long, where the water came in as at a mole hole."

Leaks were not uncommon in the days of wooden bottoms, but it should not have happened in a ship that had been supposedly reconditioned in Holland. There would seem to be good evidence that the shipwrights of Delftshaven had taken advantage of the voyagers' total ignorance of the sea and ships. But the condition of the *Speedwell* was not the only reason for the "bundle of lead" inside poor Cushman.

Christopher Martin was behaving more like a dictator than a governor on board the *Mayflower*. "He so insulteth over our poor people, with such scorn and contempt, as if they were not good enough to wipe his shoes," Cushman lamented. "It would break your heart to see his dealing, and the mourning of our people; they complain to me and alas I can do nothing for them. If I speak to him, he flies in my face as mutinous, and says no complaints shall be heard or received but by himself, and says they are forward and waspish, discontented people, and I do ill to hear them."

The passengers were not the only ones Martin was enraging, according to Cushman. "The sailors also are so offended at his ignorant boldness in meddling and controlling in things he knows not what belongs to as that some threaten to mischief him; others say they will leave the ship and go their way." A number of the passengers were having similar thoughts, and Martin forbade them to go ashore at Dartmouth.

"Friend," wrote Cushman, summing it all up, "if ever we make a plantation, God works a miracle, especially considering how scant we shall be of victuals and most of all disunited amongst ourselves and devoid of good tutors and regiment. . . . If I should write to you of all things which promiscuously forerun our ruin, I should overcharge my weak head and grieve your tender heart. Only this, I pray you prepare for evil tidings of us every day."

As for his own fate, Cushman could only report that poor William Ring (another victim of mal de mer) "and myself do strive who shall be meat first for the fishes; but we look for a glorious resurrection."

After at least four days, and possibly a week, they put to sea again, the *Speedwell's* obvious leaks repaired and her rigging and sails again readjusted according to the best advice they could get in Dartmouth. This time, surely, they were on their way. Out of the Channel into the heaving swells of the Atlantic they plowed. Land's End and the Scilly Islands fell behind them, and they were almost three hundred miles across the mighty ocean when Captain Reynolds was told by an alarmed mate that the water was rising in the *Speedwell's* hold once more, and the men were ordered to the pumps.

Another hour and the pumpers reported that they were barely staying even with the rising flood. Regretfully, Reynolds had to inform William Bradford that it was suicide to go any farther. Once more the signal of distress was made, and once more the captain of the *Speedwell* put off in his boat to confer with Captain Jones aboard the *Mayflower*. The grim decision was quickly reached: turn back again.

This time they limped into Plymouth, a few miles closer to the Atlantic on the same English coast. It was a slow return. The *Speedwell* had to shorten sail drastically, since with full sail the masts put extra strain on the already opened timbers. If a sudden "breather," as the furious southwest storms were called along that shore, had come roaring down on them, the *Speedwell* would have certainly gone to the bottom with all hands. But the weather remained merciful, and after perhaps another week of sailing, the two ships limped into Plymouth harbor.

The choice of Plymouth showed that Jones knew his business. The town was famous for its shipbuilders and had a full supply of experts to examine the recalcitrant *Speedwell*. A witness from another voyage of the time told of such anatomy work on cranky vessels. "There might be seen master, master's mate, boatswain, quartermaster, coopers, carpenters and who not, with candles in their hands, creeping along the ribs viewing the sides and searching every corner and listening in every place if they could hear the water run."

The performance was repeated on the *Speedwell* for days on end, but the frustrating little ship refused to show a single leak that could be blamed and repaired. Finally, the assembled experts reluctantly pronounced her basically unseaworthy. "The general weakness of the ship," is how William Bradford describes it. Apparently the new masts that had been stepped into the *Speedwell* in Holland were too large, and when running in the heavy Atlantic swell with a full suit of sails, they would "work" the ship until the strained timbers opened wider and wider. There was nothing to do but abandon her, the men of Plymouth told the dismayed voyagers.

This was a catastrophic blow. Delays and disagreements were frustrating but hardly struck at the fundamental plans of the expedition. The *Speedwell* was the cornerstone of these plans. Without her, any hope of large profits dwindled away and the isolation of the colony would be complete. There would be no way to get messages to England if supplies ran short, or to return sick and discontented citizens. Moreover, if they were to go forward now, it would have to be on the *Mayflower* alone.

Visions of the disastrous Blackwell voyage of the previous year instantly rose before everyone's eyes. Was God trying to warn them, with these mishaps, that an equally horrible doom was waiting for them out there on the Atlantic, or in the New World? For people who tried to find in everyday events the finger of God's guidance, it was no small question. There were long hours of meditation and of conferences between themselves and with Captain Christopher Jones. What did the captain think of attempting the Atlantic alone?

Jones told them he had confidence in his ship, his crew, and himself. As for crossing alone, dozens of ships had done it.

True enough, but the loners were largely fishermen, with no one aboard to feed but their crews. The other colonizing expeditions had all sailed in groups of two and three ships or more. Being blown a thousand miles off course or drifting for days in a dead calm were constant possibilities. With a hundred passengers to feed, supplies could vanish. For the landsman, the presence of other ships was a small reassurance that if the one he was aboard got in trouble, it did not mean the end.

Christopher Jones's calm confidence was born of thousands of hours at sea. For those to whom the land was more familiar, facing the Atlantic in a single ship could not have been a pleasant thought. But after more prayer and meditation, the voyagers found their courage was "answerable." They decided, in William Bradford's words, to "proceed with the other ship. The which (though it was grievous and caused great discouragement) was put into execution."

Supplies were lugged from the *Speedwell* to the *Mayflower*. Captain Jones meanwhile worked out the maximum number he could take aboard without unnecessary danger. They were not going to repeat Blackwell's fatal overcrowding. About twenty passengers would have to be sent back.

With what had already happened, it was not especially difficult to find twenty more than willing to turn around. "Those that went back were for the most part such as were willing so to do, either out of some discontent or fear they conceived of the ill success of the voyage," William Bradford says, "seeing so many crosses befall, and the year time so far spent. But others in regard of their own weakness and charge of many young children were thought least useful and most unfit to bear the brunt of this hard adventure; unto which work of God, and judgment of their brethren, they were contented to submit." Among those who were most willing to stay home was Robert Cushman and his family. Seasickness and forebodings of disaster had taken their toil. "Heart and courage was gone from them," Bradford says.

The *Speedwell* returned to London with the twenty dischargees. There, she would be taken over by Weston and his fellow merchants, sold at a loss, and, as Bradford writes with chagrin, "put into her old trim, she made many voyages and performed her service very sufficiently to the great profit of her owners." Bradford casts some severe aspersions on the character of Captain Reynolds, accusing him of deliberately piling sail on the *Speedwell* to make her seams open, because he and his crew wanted to escape their contract to stay a year in the New World. "They plotted this stratagem, to free themselves; as afterwards was known and by some of them confessed," Bradford says. It is possible, but it is equally possible that Reynolds wanted to make sure he had a sound ship before he got too far out on the Atlantic.

Whatever the truth of the *Speedwell's* collapse, she was lost. The exiles faced the Atlantic, and the wilderness, without her. "Like Gideon's army," Bradford writes, "this small number was divided, as if the Lord by this work of His Providence thought these few too many for the great work He had to do." Only such profound faith could find optimism in what had befallen the expedition thus far. By now it was September 6. They could look forward to arriving on a savage coast at the beginning of winter. It was over seven weeks since the *Mayflower* had sailed from London, six since the *Speedwell* had left Delftshaven. They had already consumed all the provisions they had calculated for their voyage. Now they were eating food that they might need to stay alive after they landed.

Their only consolation was the friendly treatment they

had received from the Plymouth shipwrights and other citizens who had offered them the hospitality of the town. They had also had some interesting conversations with Sir Ferdinando Gorges, the governor of Plymouth and head of the Council for New England. He had assured them that the company expected to receive its royal charter any day now, and urged them to give up their plans for the mouth of Hudson's River and select any place they chose in New England. He would confirm their rights instantly, and back them up with all the resources his company could muster. The colonists had listened politely and said they would give the matter further consideration on their voyage. But privately they still preferred to trust the patent they had in hand rather than one that might or might not be lurking in the royal bush.

So "all being compact together in one ship," Bradford says, "they put to sea again with a prosperous wind." This time there were no loving tears or well-wishing prayers to see them on their way. One writer has imagined a conversation between a townsman and one of the *Mayflower's* crew a few days before they sailed:

"Who are they folk? What seek they?"

"Mark ye, I know only they be in part puke stocking louts, for to dig in the ground, and part psalmsingers, what pray day and night."

"Ye go on wages, or shares?"

"By Gys, on wages, man! There'll be no shares, ha! ha!"

It may well have happened. By now the superstitious sailors must have been convinced that these "psalmsingers" were hopelessly hexed. As for the rest of England, they did not even give them a passing thought. In London they were talking about King James's deplorable weakness in dealing with Spain. The Thirty Years' War, which was to reduce Germany's population by one-third before it was over, had begun in Bohemia, and now Spain had entered the conflict on the side of the Catholics, sending an army rampaging through the Palatinate of the Rhine, which was ruled by James's Protestant son-in-law Frederick. The English court was in an uproar, with the king hysterically denouncing Spain and vowing that the long-talked-of marriage between the Spanish infanta and Charles, the Prince of Wales, was forever canceled. Along Holland's borders, Spain was readying more legions for another assault on the Dutch Republic. With Europe about to go up in flames, who could stop to notice a handful of tattered exiles sailing west in a weather-beaten freighter, under the absurd delusion that God would somehow protect them in their amateur assault on a wilderness that had already defeated thousands of tougher, better equipped pioneers?

Chapter 5

EVEN SAILORS PRAYED

A "fine small gale" blowing east by northeast sent the *Mayflower* bounding out upon the North Atlantic at a six- or seven-knot pace. It was a welcome gift, but it had its dark side. Almost everyone promptly became seasick as the old ship pitched and rolled through the swells. With sanitation facilities limited to buckets and 102 passengers, including some 34 children aboard, life belowdeck must have been anything but pleasant.

No one knows exactly how the voyagers arranged themselves on the *Mayflower*, but there have been some good educated guesses. To get an adequate picture, we must first take another look at the ship herself. As a freighter, she was built for roominess and carrying capacity. From the center of her taffrail on the stern to the end of the "beak" under the bowsprit forward, she measured about 113 feet. Between the deep hold and the upper deck was a gun deck about twenty-six feet wide and seventy-eight feet long. It was here that most of the passengers were settled. From the gun deck the *Mayflower's* sides "tumbled" in until she was only nineteen feet wide on her upper deck.

Forward on the upper deck was the forecastle, where the thirty-man crew lived. A good portion of it was taken up by the galley, and the foremast was stepped through the forward end of it, not leaving much space for thirty men in a compartment that was only fourteen feet long and thirteen feet wide at one end and about seventeen feet wide at the other. But the average sailor traveled light, and at sea, half the men were always on duty.

Next came the ship's waist, the lowest part of the upper deck, where even in mild weather the spray would come gushing over. Then came the half deck, some six feet higher, and finally, up another four feet, the lofty poop deck, where the captain surveyed his domain. The house created by the half deck was called the steerage, and it was here that the helmsman stood, guiding his ship with a whipstaff, a huge lever attached to the tiller head beneath his feet. A tiny hatch above him cast light on the "bittacle" in front of him, containing the ship's two compasses. He took his orders from above, where the officer of the deck could see how the ship was heading.

Below the poop deck was the poop house, a moderately roomy cabin perhaps thirteen by seventeen, where the master's mates dined and otherwise relaxed. Directly below this was the Great Cabin, where the captain slept and ate in lonely splendor. Some writers have conjectured that the *Mayflower's* poop house was divided in half and that about eighteen passengers were accommodated here. We also suspect that Captain Jones gave up his cabin and joined his mates in the crowded quarters of the divided poop house, giving bunk room to another thirty-six adults. There were eighteen married couples and eleven unmarried girls, many in their early teens, as well as eight or ten very young children aboard. Most of these probably went into the after-house cabins, where there was some small degree of privacy. This would leave about fifty-four people to be taken care of on the gun deck, where measurements indicate there was bunk room enough for around seventy-five. These were married men without wives, bachelors, and grown boys. Some slept in the shallop, which had been divided into four parts and stowed here. Others may have had crude bunks built into the ship's sides, or imitated the sailors in their hammocks.

This may have disposed the passengers for the night, but no one sleeps twenty-four hours a day, especially children. From the first day at sea, there was friction between crew and passengers. No doubt many of them got in the way while the sailors were trying to work the ship. A square-rigger like the *Mayflower* had (to the landsman's eye) an incredible tangle of yards and lines to manipulate. As they leaped to obey a mate's order to trim a mainsail or alter a yard, the sailors did not relish tripping over children or brushing aside a gaping female. Men who had the detested graveyard watch, midnight to 4 A.M., were infuriated by the shouts and laughter of playing children during the day while they were trying to sleep.

To add to the bedlam, there were two dogs aboard, a husky mastiff belonging to Peter Brown and a small spaniel owned by John Goodman. The mastiff would be useful as a watchdog. Previous explorers had found that the Indians were easily frightened by this fierce English breed. The spaniel would seem to have been tolerated as a consolation for Goodman, who had left his bride of two months behind.

Even without the minor irritations created by dogs and children, the passengers and the crew were poorly matched. The average seaman of 1620 was an illiterate, profane brawler with nothing but contempt for landlubbers. Watching their seasick passengers staggering about the ship for the first few days hardly increased the crew's admiration, and when the passengers gathered in the *Mayflower's* waist each morning for psalms and prayers, their contempt became monumental.

Religion was synonymous with the droning sermons of the village parson and the humdrum life of the family man which they had gone to sea to escape. It was a positive affront to find piety pursuing them here on the ocean.

Muttered complaints about "glib-gabbety puke-stockings" quickly grew into outspoken mockery. The sailors took special pleasure in bawling oaths and profanities at the top of their lungs, and the ship's officers apparently made no effort to restrain them. The boatswain's mate, the man who would be closest to the able seamen and in the best position to stop them, was one of the ringleaders, taking delight in adding to the oaths a few choice selections of his own.

One sailor, described by William Bradford as a "proud and very profane young man, of a lusty able body, which made him the more haughty," was particularly nasty. "He would always be condemning the poor people in their sickness, and cursing them daily with grievous execrations, and did not let to tell them that he hoped to help to cast half of them overboard before they came to their journey's end, and make merry with what they had." The mild, peace-loving exiles simply did not know how to cope with such a character. The leaders, such as John Carver and William Brewster, "gently" reproached him. But this only made him curse and swear and taunt the passengers even more "bitterly."

They were at sea a little more than two weeks,—"before they came half seas over," in William Bradford's phrase—when this proud and profane young man was inexplicably stricken with a sudden disease. In the space of a few days, perhaps even hours, he died "in a desperate manner," raving and cursing to his last breath. One doctor who has studied the story suspects that the man succumbed to delirium tremens. He may well have broken into the ship's ample liquor supply and drunk himself to death. The other possibilities—scurvy or typhus—are ruled out because no one else was reported ill, and these two common killers of 1620 always struck in plague proportions.

The other seamen were more than a little appalled by the sudden demise of their champion. Superstitious to a man, they could not help wondering if these humble singers of psalms had some special powers or favored position with God. "It was an astonishment to all his fellows," Bradford notes with quiet satisfaction, and for the rest of the voyage no one in the crew was inclined to taunt or torment the passengers with such uninhibited malice.

By now most of the company had gotten their sea legs

and were beginning to create a routine out of the cramped monotony of shipboard life. To our eyes, used to ocean liners as tall as skyscrapers, the *Mayflower* would be little more than an oversized rowboat. But there was room enough on board for children to play such mild games as skipping rope, and a fair number of adults could enjoy the sea air on the upper decks without dangerously crowding them.

But for young married couples, such as the Bradfords, the lack of privacy must have been painful. Numerous inaccurate paintings and poems have left us with the general impression that most of these people were middle-aged or older. Actually, only four had reached their fifties—John Carver, Mr. and Mrs. Brewster, and James Chilton, the Canterbury tailor, who was the oldest at fifty-seven. Four others were in their forties, and the rest in their thirties and twenties.

But the problem of privacy was overshadowed in these first weeks by the food—once their stomachs had settled enough to taste it. The range of food available for a long voyage was not wide. The only way they could preserve meat was to pickle it in brine. Beef, pork, and fish, thus treated, were on the menu, along with biscuits made of wheat flour and dried pea flour cooked into saucer-sized discs. These were the two perennials; most ships alternated between "fish days" and "meat days." Dried ground peas were also available, and Holland cheese. Mush, oatmeal, and pease pudding were also occasionally included.

The opportunity to do any genuine cooking was practically nonexistent. The galley was barred to the passengers; with one cook to feed officers and crew—perhaps forty men

—it was impossible to undertake feeding a hundred passengers. Most of this unpalatable menu was therefore served cold, with a minimum of cooking allowed over a little "hearth-box" filled with sand, probably on a rotating-family basis.

The women may well have taken a cue from the ship's cook and served an occasional pea soup or a lobscouse, a thick soup or stew containing chunks of salt meat. Soup was always welcome aboard because it gave the diners something to soften their biscuits in—after a few weeks they became as hard as cannon balls. For a treat there may have been burgoo, oatmeal sweetened with molasses, or doughboys, dumplings of wet flour boiled in pork fat, or best of all, plum duff, a suet pudding containing raisins or prunes.

All this was washed down with quantities of beer. The crew's daily ration was a quart per man, and the voyagers probably drank that much too. No one in 1620 would drink water except as a last desperate recourse. The best medical opinion held that it was injurious to health and often fatal. Aboard ship, the opinion was well founded. Water was carried in charred casks. For the first few weeks at sea, it would stink so foully that no one could gag down a mouthful. But after another week or two it cleared and became relatively odorless, though somewhat slimy.

If the food was typical of other sailing ships, its taste and variety were not the only threats to the appetite. There were always a multitude of insects burrowing through it— little brown grubs, weevils, and maggots. Rats, too, were certain to be prevalent, especially on an old ship such as the

Mayflower, and they would also leave their unpleasant deposits in the food. Witnesses from other voyages have described sailors skimming off as many floating insects, rat offal, and maggots as they could from their lobscouse and then gratefully slurping it down.

Fortunately, there were other things to do besides lament the awful food. As soon as everyone recovered from their initial bouts of seasickness, Miles Standish began drilling squads of men in handling the guns and swords on which the colony's survival might well depend. The captain himself had a fine rapier, which he had personally shortened some six inches so that a man his size could wear it without difficulty. Most of the other swords were of the cutting type, and there was not much need to instruct anyone in their use, especially against Indians who would be without armor or swords of their own.

Far more important was instruction in handling the cumbersome matchlock muskets of 1620. These primitive weapons were over five feet long and so heavy that they were usually fired from a forked rest thrust into the ground before the gunner. The mechanism was as complicated as it was uncertain. The "match" was made of lightly woven rope soaked in niter. It was attached to a holder on the outside of the lock, known as the serpentine, which functioned as the hammer in the modern gun. When the trigger was pulled, the serpentine swung the match into the priming pan, and the gun theoretically went off.

Firing a matchlock was slow work. Again and again, Standish had his men go through the lengthy maneuver on the *Mayflower's* unsteady deck. First the match was re-

moved from the serpentine with the left hand and held between the fingers. With the thumb and forefinger of the
same hand, each man had to hold the barrel of the gun up-
right while with his right hand he poured a charge of powder down the muzzle. Next he shoved home a ball and a
wad of tow or paper with his wooden rammer. Finally the
flashpan had to be "primed" with fine-grained powder, the
cover closed, and any loose powder blown away.

Now they were ready to fire—almost. The match must
first be returned to the serpentine and adjusted. The glowing tip had to be blown into life. The match had to be
watched continually, Standish warned. If it burned down
to the serpentine, it would go out. When this happened,
it should be instantly reignited from the other end, which
was also kept burning for this reason.

Now—ready, aim carefully—fire! The crash of a dozen
muskets shook the *Mayflower*. The gunners were enveloped
in a great cloud of smoke. Not wanting to waste precious
powder, Standish probably had the men go through the monotonous drill more often than he had them fire, but they had
to shoot the guns once or twice to get used to their tremendous kick. An unprepared man could easily dislocate his
shoulder.

A few men on board, Miles Standish and probably Stephen Hopkins, had more modern guns—snaphaunce or
flintlock muskets, which could be fired without the clumsy
match and which were far more accurate. They were also
more expensive, and most of the voyagers had had to content themselves with the second-rate matchlocks.

Military preparations were by no means the only concern

of the leaders from Leyden. The future organization of the colony was a far bigger question. They were acutely aware that they were a minority—a mere twenty-seven adults— yet it was vital to retain control of the group if they were to find the kind of commonwealth they envisioned. As a first step in this direction, when they lost the *Speedwell* they deposed Christopher Martin from his post as "governor" of the *Mayflower* and elected John Carver in his place. But when they landed they would need allies among the "strangers"—and a good part of these first weeks were spent in cautious attempts to get acquainted and find out who was trustworthy.

Stephen Hopkins was a man who automatically commanded respect, but he was a difficult, contentious character with an alarming past record of dissension. When he had been shipwrecked in Bermuda in 1609, he had come within a whisker of being hanged for mutiny. Richard Warren of London was called "master," a social term only slightly below "gentleman," and seemed to be a serious, dependable man. So was William Mullins. Then there was Christopher Martin, whose disposition showed no sign of changing, and the Billington family, who were uncooperative about everything, full of complaints about food and sleeping quarters, quarreling with crew and fellow passengers alike. It was not going to be easy to control such a mixed company.

William Brewster had worked as a teacher in Holland, and he may have set up a school for the children on the *Mayflower*. As charming as he was gentle, with a disposition William Bradford describes as always "cheerful," Brewster was the perfect man for the job. He had brought along a library of almost two hundred books, which he no doubt doled out to all comers. But every family had at least one book of its own—the Geneva translation of the Holy Bible—and it was this that Brewster used for a schoolbook.

For the older boys and young men such as John Alden, there were wrestling matches and other sports with the sailors. On another voyage a few years later, one diarist noted how "the Captain set children and grown men to harmless exercises which the seamen were very active in and did our people much good." The stronger, such as Alden, may well have pitched in with the crew to haul on the thick and cumbersome halyards as one of the ship's six sails were dropped or hoisted. The huge bulky sails required backbreaking effort to maneuver.

From his poop deck Christopher Jones surveyed the life below him with a captain's uncompromising eye. Day and night the decks had to be swabbed, the sails and lines mended, and the sailors kept at the perpetual task of keeping their clothes and themselves reasonably clean. Any sickness or breach of discipline on the part of passengers or crew was reported to him immediately.

The ship itself required constant attention. Sails rubbing against the rigging could be holed, and ropes could part in the same way within a matter of hours. As the wind shifted, the sails had to be expertly handled to get the maximum benefit from it. If it blew aft to forward, both sheet lines would be well slacked out on port and starboard sides so that the sails could stretch to maximum width and drive the ship at her best speed. But the wind was seldom so cooperative, and when it shifted to dead ahead, the sails would flap and lose all their driving power, so the course had to be altered—the nautical word is tacking—until the sails filled again. When the wind came on either quarter, the sails had to be adjusted once more to get the most out of it.

As the absolute ruler of this floating kingdom, Captain Jones had chosen their current route. They were not going to follow the old sea trail blazed by Columbus, which ran past the Canaries, on a great southerly loop down to the West Indies, and then north along the American coast. It was a thousand miles longer and, for a single ship, far more dangerous. Spanish, French, and Algerian pirates lurked along it, always ready to pounce on a lone ship, especially if she was English.

Jones had decided to hold the *Mayflower* firm on the forty-second parallel and drive for the New World on an almost straight line. It was a route lately preferred by the English, but neither Jones nor his fellow captains knew that almost all the way across, they were bucking the contrary current of the Gulf Stream, which slowed the ship's speed to a bare two miles an hour.

To tell him where he was on the trackless ocean, Captain Jones relied largely on shooting the sun with his cross-staff, a graduated bar of wood about thirty-six inches long, across which at right angles was attached a sliding bar about twenty-six inches long; there were sights on one end of the vertical bar and on both ends of the horizontal bar. By measuring the angle between the sun and the horizon through these sights, Jones was able to approximate his latitude pretty well, but of longitude he was almost always in the dark. The modern chronometer, by which today's nav-igators determine their distance east or west of Greenwich meridian with marvelous accuracy, would not be aboard ships at sea for a long time.

For judging his speed, Captain Jones had only two crude instruments, the log line and the log glass. The log line was a quadrant of wood weighted on one side with a line about 150 fathoms long attached to it. The line was knotted at regular intervals, and by counting how many knots ran out while the sand ran through the log glass, the number of knots, or miles per hour, could be roughly computed. In heavy weather, or when fighting head winds, the device was almost useless, however.

Heavy weather was exactly what Captain Jones and his mates were expecting. Balmy breezes could not last at this season of the year on the Atlantic. Again and again, second mate Robert Coppin, who had been transferred from the *Speedwell,* or first mate John Clark would stare grimly into the northwestern horizon where the westerlies came roaring down from Greenland. Or they would quietly study the sur-face of the ocean looking for that "head sea" which often announces the gale hours before it arises, with the regular heave of swell upon mounting swell.

Finally it came, the cold breath of the Arctic, tearing down the long reach of white-capped sea. "All hands, all hands," roared the boatswain's mate, adding some choice persuasion which must have made the passengers shudder. "Up, up, you gobbets, you abbey-lubbers!" Into the shrouds went the shivering seamen, some of them still half asleep, while others heaved on the groaning, squealing yards. Aboard the old square-riggers, sails were furled by hoisting, never an easy job, and worse now with the wind tearing at them. Then came the job of lashing them, sixty feet above the careening ocean.

Beneath the feet and before the eyes of the horrified passengers the *Mayflower* suddenly began behaving in a new and entirely alarming manner. The masts swayed crazily against the lowering sky, and the bow lifted hesitantly over first one swell and then a second, and finally a third gave her no chance to come up and she plowed into the heart of the onrushing mountain of water, which came thundering over the forecastle and inundated the waist. A terrific shudder ran through the *Mayflower*. She was "hawse full," water pouring off her waist and streaming through her forecastle, where the cook was frantically shutting portholes.

Now sea after sea broke over the old ship, sending her reeling first to the port and then to the starboard, while men at the whipstaff fought to keep her headed. On the poop deck, Captain Jones and his mates, drenched in flying spray, bellowed more orders to the men aloft.

If there were any civilians left on deck, Captain Jones surely chased them with a roar: "All passengers below!" Hatches were secured, portholes on the gun decks bolted tight, cannon and any other heavy movables lashed down. Captain Jones and his crew were left alone abovedeck to cope with their natural enemy, the ocean. "We shall have wind," Captain John Smith wrote in his advice to would-be explorers. "Take in the sprit sail. In with your top sails. Lower your main sails, lower the foresail. . . . Lash sure the ordnance, strike your top masts to the cap. . . . How capes the ship? Con the ship, spoon before the wind. She lists! She lies under the sea. Try her with a cross jack, bowse it up with the outlooker. She will founder in the sea!"

Not if Christopher Jones could help it. He had done all these things, and more. But it was as bad a storm as he had ever seen. Every inch of sail had to be furled. There was nothing to do but hull—run before the wind with bare poles —even though they were being driven hundreds of miles off their course. Still the Atlantic pounded after them, foaming over the lower decks, flinging great geysers of spray over the poop, while on the howling wind came the bitter autumn rain, cutting through the thin shirts and trousers of the sailors.

Belowdeck the passengers huddled together praying for God's help. On other voyages, the women passengers had panicked in similar storms, making everyone "look one upon the other with troubled hearts and fainting bosoms, our clamors drowned in the winds." To make matters worse, if possible, after the first day or two the *Mayflower* proved herself a wet ship. The pounding seas opened all the seams in her upper works, and with every wave, freezing water cascaded down upon the hapless passengers, huddled below in the foul semidarkness, lit only by the occasional glow of a single candle through panes of opaque lanthorn. Knowing nothing of seamanship, they felt that every roll and pitch and shudder of the ship was the end, as well it might be.

Stephen Hopkins must have remembered with special alarm another wild storm, which had sent him and others aboard the *Sea Adventure* piling onto the Bermuda reefs in

1609. One of his fellow passengers left a vivid description of that fierce blow, and many of the details were probably repeated upon the *Mayflower*. "Our sails wound up, lay without their use, and if at any time we bore but a hullock, or half forecourse, to guide her before the sea, six and sometimes eight men were not enough to hold the whipstaff in the steerage." Once, a wave "broke upon the poop and . . . covered our ship from stern to stern, like a garment of vast clouds it filled her brim full, from the hatches up to the spar deck."

Even a moderate storm—winds up to fifty miles an hour —piles up waves fifty feet high, and the winds that struck the *Mayflower* at this time of the year on the North Atlantic were at least of this velocity. Anyone who has ever watched a ship at sea fight her way through a gale can have some small idea of what Captain Jones and his men went through watching waves roar down upon them as high as the masts, seeing the weary ship plunging down, down into immense hollows of water, and fighting her way up the other side, while the foaming ocean stormed over every inch of her decks. Again and again, the waves pounded down on her, great smashing blows of the Atlantic's inexhaustible fist.

At such times even sailors prayed, and William Brewster must have reminded the passengers of the voyage some of them had made from England to Holland in 1609. Their ship had been driven almost to the coast of Norway by a fantastic storm, and "when the water ran into their mouths and ears," the captain and crew had given up in despair, crying: "We sink, we sink." But the exiles had cried out: "Yet Lord thou canst save, Yet Lord thou canst save," and miraculously, so it had seemed to them—and to the awed sailors—the wind had soon slackened and they were able to limp into Holland, weary but alive. Elder Brewster urged his damp and frightened friends to call on God again with the same faith.

Someone suggested a psalm. Yes, a psalm, let us all sing a psalm! Feebly the voices rose above the monstrous wind:

> Jehovah feedeth me, I shall not lack
> In grassy folds he down dooth make me lye
> He gently leads me quiet waters by
> He dooth return my soul; for his name sake
> In paths of justice leads me quietly
>
> Yea though I walk in dale of deadly-shade
> Ile fear none ill; for with me thou wilt be
> Thy rod thy staff eke, they shall comfort me.
> Fore me, a table thou has ready-made
> In their presence that my distressers be.

But still the wind thundered and the ocean smashed at their ship. Then, as their quaking voices began the next verse, another monstrous wave boomed down, and with the crash of a cannon shot, a main beam amidship cracked and buckled.

Chapter 6

WATER WATER
EVERYWHERE

Pandemonium now, both from men and weather. The captain and mates rushed below to gaze up from the gun deck at the sagging beam, the splintered deck around it. Water gushed through new openings, and the terrified passengers huddled against the ship's sides to escape it. The carpenter was summoned. What could be done? Nothing, unless they could force that beam back in place. The strongest men aboard—John Alden, the blasphemous boatswain's mate, and a half dozen others—put their shoulders to the job while the freezing water poured down on them. But it was like trying to raise the roof beam of a house. The massive piece of timber only sagged a little more. A spare beam was dragged up from the hold, and the men tried using that as a ram. Again, failure.

Then someone remembered a "great iron screw" they had bought in Holland to help them raise houses in the New World. Maybe it would do the job. Sailors and passengers

went scrambling into the hold, flinging aside boxes and
bales until they found the gleam of metal in the flickering
lantern light. Grunting and gasping, they lugged the screw
up to the gun deck and placed it under the ruined beam.
Slowly now, twist the crank, make sure the face is aimed
precisely at the break, now, put your backs into it, one two
three, it's going up, it's working! Ram that spare beam
under it, now. There!

It held. Disaster was no longer imminent. But the wind
still howled like the voice of doom, and the sea still smashed
down on the *Mayflower*. Before their eyes the splintered
deck shivered and trembled, and another cascade of water
poured down. How long would this repair job last?

This was a question that Captain Jones and his mates
must decide, and they retired to their cabin for a conference. On the gun deck, the carpenter and some sailors put
additional braces under the cracked beam, and from their
mutterings it soon became obvious to the passengers that
survival was by no means certain. "There was great distrac-
tion and difference of opinion amongst the mariners themselves," Bradford tells us. Some were for going forward, but
their motives were far from reassuring. If they turned back
now, halfway over, they would break their contract, forfeit
their wages—and it was almost as long one way as the
other. Still, some were for turning back because, in Bradford's words, "they were loath to hazard their lives too desperately."

Alarmed, William Bradford, William Brewster and John
Carver sought out Captain Jones and his mates and asked
them bluntly whether they were in serious danger. Was this

the first of many possible cracks in the old *Mayflower?* If they sailed on would the next break or the one after it spell disintegration? If so, let us run for the nearest land. Africa, the Canary Islands—anywhere.

All eyes turned to Captain Jones. The mates had given their opinions, but they did not really count. It was the captain who must decide—and 150 lives hung in the balance between his courage and his prudence. Now Christopher Jones spoke in the proud tradition of his Harwich ancestors. True, wind and weather would be more favorable on a run back to England. They could run for Africa or the Canaries, which were even closer. But the old ship was still solid under the water, and that was what counted. He had seen her through bad weather before. Once, in a storm off Norway, they had had to jettison half the cargo, but the *Mayflower* had come through. She was a solid, dependable old girl, and he was ready to swear by her for a few more years, at least.

As for the splintered deck, they would caulk it as soon as the weather eased and they could melt some pitch. It would keep some of the water out, and even if the cracks opened again in a few days, as the ship worked in the wind, there was no special danger in that, as long as they did not strain things with too much sail.

A deep sigh of relief ran through the listening passengers. They had spoken out of their responsibility for the women and children below. But the problems of turning back were almost as harrowing as the risks of going forward. It was good to let this sturdy man of the sea make the decision for them. "So," William Bradford says, "they committed themselves to the will of God, and resolved to proceed."

But if they had met old Neptune's harshest challenge, the water god was still in a turbulent mood. Day after day the ship continued to wallow through mountainous seas, sometimes pounded by gales, sometimes merely hounded by typical North Atlantic weather. By now it had been weeks since anyone had been able to light a fire. The food being brought up from the hold was getting worse and worse. The biscuits had to be pounded to pieces with a chisel, the cheese was moldy, the butter rancid. Peas and grain had more and more crawling things in them. The endless slices of salt meat and fish had to be choked down or sloshed down with beer, which was also going sour.

Day after day they asked the captain or one of the mates if they could go up on deck, and the answer was always no. Too dangerous. Seas were still running as high as the poop. Even with lifelines strung, the crew had to watch the water or go overboard. So the voyagers were condemned to more hours in the foul darkness of the gun deck. A hundred people crowded into a space not much roomier in total square feet than a modern house, unable to change their clothes or wash for over thirteen weeks now, with freezing sea water sloshing and dripping around them until everyone was permanently damp and chilled.

It was enough to make anyone wonder if they were all mad to have left those warm, neat houses in Leyden, where life had flowed past as placidly as a Dutch canal. For a young girl like Dorothy Bradford, raised from early childhood in the comfortable world of the Netherlands, the question came again and again, a nagging, tormenting finger of doubt which no prayer seemed to dispel.

For the younger men, bursting with energy and vitality, the confinement belowdeck was almost intolerable. It was like a prison sentence. Who was that captain, where did he get the authority to pen us up like a cargo of animals? This was what young John Howland, hired as John Carver's servant, kept thinking. Finally he could stand it no longer. He shoved open a hatch grate and stepped out on deck. Oh, clean, delicious air! What did it matter if those waves were higher than he had ever seen water before? The simple joy of breathing made it worth the chance he was taking.

For ten or twenty seconds, this ecstasy persisted. Then a blast of wind tore at the *Mayflower*, and she heeled over like a toy ship in a tub. John Howland's feet were suddenly where his head had been, and then he was deep in the foaming frigid Atlantic. He did what every man who has ever gone overboard in the history of the sea has done. His frantic outstretched arms clutched at life, his fingers clawed at the roaring water, remembering solidity. Usually the clutching hands find only emptiness. But John Howland was one of the rare lucky ones. His hands found rope. So far over had the ship rolled that her topsail halyards were running in the water, and John Howland grabbed them and hung on.

But life was by no means certain yet. The ship was still heaving and bucking through a huge sea, and Howland found himself far beneath the wild waves. The wet ropes tore his hands; his lungs began to fill with terrible pain. Then air! The seamen of the *Mayflower* may have been a blasphemous, brawling lot, but they knew their jobs. A team of deck apes had leaped to the halyards and hauled Howland to the surface. Now he was in danger of getting his brains beaten out against the ship's hull, as the maddened sea flung him back and forth like a piece of bait on a line. But he hung on somehow, while the men above him shouted their encouragement. One sailor tied a line around his waist and teetered over the side with a boat hook in his hand. One pass, two, got him! Up on deck came John Howland like a large flounder.

He had swallowed an unpleasant amount of sea water and was half frozen. The sailors lugged him below, and for the next several days, Howland was a very sick young man. Fortunately, he had a rugged physique, and was soon downing his share of beer and salt pork again. But he had lost all his enthusiasm for the cool, clear air of the open decks—and so had everyone else. The Atlantic raged on, and its wet miserable victims did nothing but endure it.

Then a new crisis. Cries of pain from the Great Cabin. Elizabeth Hopkins was in labor. Neither she nor her husband ever expected to have their child during an Atlantic gale. By every sane calculation, they should have been in the New World by now, safely ensconced in a warm house. But it was too late to mutter regrets or make accusations. Experienced older women, such as Mary Brewster and Catherine Carver, rushed to her side. They had assisted at dozens of births during the years at Leyden, and they gave the young and frightened mother badly needed reassurance.

Hours passed with nothing but the sounds of the storm to fill the minds of those waiting on the gun deck. Childbirth was dangerous enough, but in a damp, foul cabin, without heat or warm water—no, it was better not to think about what might happen. William Brewster suggested they join in prayers for Elizabeth Hopkins, and the Leyden exiles and the London strangers knelt together while the quiet, steady voice of the ruling elder led them in asking help for the lonely woman in the aftercabin.

Then Mary Brewster strode out of the shadows holding a small bundle in her arms. A lusty yowling baby boy, Master Hopkins! Listen to him outshout the gale! A veritable son of Neptune! Stephen Hopkins agreed and promptly named the new arrival Oceanus.

The birth cheered everyone. They had snatched another life from the hungry Atlantic. Even the sailors regarded it as a good omen, and vowed that land could not be far away now. But a week and then another week passed, and nothing broke the monotony of wind and rain, cold and damp. Susanna White, also big with child, began to fret and worry. She would like to have her baby on familiar mother earth.

Dorothy Bradford was a good friend of Susanna's and did her best to make life a little easier for her. She watched five-year-old Resolved White, doing her best to save his mother unnecessary steps, made doubly dangerous in the pitching, rolling ship. But everytime Dorothy saw the youngster exchange a hug with his mother or run to her with a complaint, an aching emptiness tormented her. Resolved was the same age as her son John. Better not to have him on this miserable ship, of course. But without him she was only half a woman. All through those years at Leyden he had been hers. He had barely seen his father, toiling those endless hours over his weaving. Five was the worst possible age to separate them. If they had waited another year or two, he would have been old enough to understand.

Again Dorothy Bradford prayed for help, for the banishment of these dark and futile thoughts. But these thoughts were almost preferable to the smelly, splashing semidarkness in which she had been imprisoned for the last eight weeks. She could not share her feelings with her husband It was his decision to leave young John behind. To complain would sound like a reproach—and a good Christian wife obeyed her husband, in body and mind and soul.

The Atlantic was not through with them yet. As the tenth week at sea drew to a close, William Butten, a husky twenty-two-year-old hired as a servant for Dr. Samuel Fuller, took to his bunk complaining of a terrible weakness. One moment he was pouring sweat, unable to tolerate a blanket over him, the next he was shivering with a tremendous chill. Then came agonizing pain, stabbing lances of fire in his arms and legs, and a terrible, nameless fear.

The lad was from Austerfield, William Bradford's home village. William Brewster had probably induced him to come along during his sojourn in the north the year before. Both men felt personally responsible for him and did everything they could to comfort him. They summoned Samuel Fuller, their own doctor, and Giles Heale, the ship's surgeon, for advice. Captain Jones, who had seen more sickness at sea than both doctors, also came down for a look.

All shook their heads. It was the first case of scurvy. Hardly surprising, in a voyage that was already a month overdue. Butten had come aboard the *Mayflower* in London, and had been eating the miserable diet of salt meat, biscuit, and dried peas for seventeen weeks now. He was a young man with no one to watch his diet for him, and he may have disliked the lemon juice and dried fruit recommended by shipboard veterans as an antidote to scurvy. There was nothing to do now but force a little of these remedies into him—though it may well be too late.

The next morning, Butten's breathing became labored. He was still in terrible pain, and now he had to fight for every breath. William Bradford sent his wife hurrying to Dr. Samuel Fuller. The diagnosis was grim. Butten had pneumonia as well. All afternoon, the trapped voyagers sat in the darkness listening to his rasping struggle for life. William Brewster led them in prayers once more. But this time the Atlantic would not be denied. Before morning Butten was dead.

Quickly, the matter-of-fact sailors sewed him into his shroud. Dead men were not allowed to linger aboard a ship at sea. They spread infection and, in the superstitious conviction of salt-water men, slowed down the ship. As dawn broke over the heaving, sullen ocean, William Butten of Austerfield, almost three thousand miles from those green fields which he and William Bradford called home, plunged into the gray depths.

For William Bradford and his friends, it was a time for prayer and pleading. This death would be the first of many if they did not get off the *Mayflower* soon. Belowdeck there were ominous signs of trouble. Men were complaining of swollen legs; one or two women were in their bunks with William Butten's chills and torpor. The male servants, both the young men and boys, were particularly bad. Like Butten, they had probably been careless of their diets, and they also lacked the sense of purpose that sustained the family men. How much longer, how much longer? the leaders asked Christopher Jones. The captain took them into his cabin and showed them his charts. By the crude calculations of the log line, landfall could come at any time. According to his cross-staff, he was back on the 42nd parallel. But he could not press on too much sail, with his weakened deck. They must somehow content themselves with their creeping pace.

More days slipped by. The weather at last became bearable. Hatches were opened, and those who were well walked the narrow decks once more. On the captain's advice, even those who were sick in their bunks were routed out and forced to take some exercise.

There was an air of expectancy quivering through the ship. Aloft in the crows'-nest a lookout peered endlessly over the western horizon. Nothing rose there but more and more miles of trackless ocean. Another day of creeping. Would it ever end? Another night below in the smelly bunks, restless sleep broken by whimperings of unhappy children, the moans of the feverish.

Morning on November 9 was no different from the other mornings since they had come aboard. Abovedeck the crew plodded through their routines. Captain Jones leaned over the taffrail of his poop deck watching the dawn grow on the glistening sea. Out of the west came a curious gull, to dip and weave above the weary freighter with astonished cries. An old salt scrubbing down the half-deck vowed he could *smell* land. The last pale quarter of the old moon drooped in the dawning sky as the lookout scrambled to his perch in the rigging.

Above, the sails flapped in the dying wind. Mate John Clark pointed to the changing color of the water—indigo blue had blended into emerald. Another good sign. Land was close, and they had better begin to take soundings. The captain agreed, and sent the leadsman to his place outside the mizzen shrouds. In a few moments the hiss and plop of the lead line was followed by the singsong call of twenty, thirty, forty, fifty fathoms. Then a sudden break in the sleepy chant and the excited bellow: "And bottom at eighty fathoms, sir!"

Land. It was there, beneath the *Mayflower's* encrusted keel, the continent of North America, reaching out into the sea to welcome them. Captain Christopher Jones looked around him at his old enemy, the mighty Atlantic, and mocked him with a victorious smile.

Now the sun was making the ship's worn sails gleam as if woven with gold. A breath of wind came on the spreading light, and the sails stopped their flapping and began to fill. Then from the maintop lookout burst the cry that passengers and crew had been hearing in their dreams for weeks.

LA-A-ND HO! LA-A-ND HO!

Chapter 7

WHAT COULD NOW
SUSTAIN THEM?

Sleepy men and women stumbled from their bunks, still not sure whether they had heard it or dreamed it. No, there it was again: LAND. LAND HO! Up the ladders to the main deck they streamed, refusing to believe until they saw it for themselves. "Where away?" bellowed Captain Jones.

"Two points on the weather bow, sir!"

All eyes followed the captain, and there, looming out of the ocean as if it were being created by the rays of the rising sun, was a long low stretch of brown and gray, a faceless world, but real. Ding dong, ding dong, ding dong went the ship's bell. It was seven o'clock on the morning of November 9. They were sixty-five days out from Plymouth, ninety-seven from Southampton.

Shouts of joy and tears of relief mingled. Many fell on their knees and thanked God with simple spontaneity. William Brewster suggested a song of gladness and gratitude,

and in a few moments from the crowded waist of the *Mayflower* soared the words of Psalm 100.

> Shout to Jehovah, all the earth
>   Serve you Jehovah with gladness
> Before him come with singing mirth
>   Know that Jehovah he God is
> It's he that made us, not we
>   His folk and sheep of his feeding
> O with confession enter ye
>   His gates, his courtyards with praising.
> Confess to him, bless you his name
>   Because Jehovah he good is
> His mercy ever is the same
>   And his faith, unto all ages.

But rejoicing must be brief. The *Mayflower* was under
way now, moving steadily closer to this unknown coast. A
hurried conference with Captain Jones was in order. Where
were they? What part of North America was this? If his
charts and his navigation were correct, Jones told them,
this long, low shore was part of that great arm of land
known as Cape Cod. Captain John Smith, charting the coast
six years before, had renamed it Cape James, after the king,
but most sailors still preferred the original christening, in
memory of the magnificent fishing off its shores.

All very well, but the territory of the Virginia Company,
in which their patent entitled them to settle, did not extend
north of latitude 41—present day Westchester County, New
York. In John Carver's baggage were letters from Sir Edwin
Sandys and John Ferrar, Treasurer and Secretary of the
Virginia Company, introducing them to Sir George Yeard-
ley, Governor of Jamestown, and admonishing this gentle-

man "that he should give them the best advice he could for trading in Hudson's River."

These were legal facts and potential advantages that could not be ignored. But the *Mayflower's* passengers were also men who believed strongly in the personal guidance of God. They could not avoid noticing that the winds had carried them to that very New England coast that Weston and his associates had urged them to choose. No English bishops to worry about here (a potential problem in Virginia Company territory). At Plymouth, Sir Ferdinando Gorges had assured them that his Council for New England would promptly issue them a patent. Sickness was a growing threat, sea weariness was universal. Perhaps it would be wiser to land here.

How far was it to Hudson's River, they asked Jones? About fifteen leagues—sixty miles—according to his maps. Another day or two of sailing. After some hesitation and debate, the passengers decided to rely on the patent they had in their hands, rather than one Sir Ferdinando Gorges might —or might not—be able to issue them in the uncertain future. Tack about and head south, they told Captain Jones. They would grit their teeth and endure the *Mayflower* for a few more days.

By now they were close enough to see high brown bluffs and the tops of tall trees. But it was all in outline. The ship's master did not dare venture too close to shore in these crudely charted seas. He knew from the experience of other sailors that there was some very ugly water off this stretch of coast. Captain John Smith had described "long and dangerous shoals and rocks." Captain Bartholomew Gosnold and his men had made almost the same landfall in 1602, and within a matter of hours were wishing they were a thousand leagues at sea again. They had encountered miles of shoals and breakers which they named "Tucker's Terror," in honor of one of their mates who was apparently the most frightened man aboard.

Up in the bow, the leadsman was hard at work feeling for the bottom. "Forty fathoms, thirty fathoms, twenty fathoms." They were losing water all the time. With a loaded ship drawing some twelve feet, Captain Jones could not be too careful. They were using a hand lead now, weighing some fourteen pounds, easier to haul up than the hundred-pound dipsey with which they had begun their sounding.

For half the day they continued this cautious progress down the coast. The leadsman's chant began to lull everyone into sleepy security. They were rolling along in comfortably safe water, though fighting a tide that slowed them to a crawl. Then from the maintop lookout came a sudden shout: "Breakers ahead!" All hands peered in the direction of his pointing hand and saw white, churning water, miles of it—shoal water, ready and able to pound the bottom out of the *Mayflower*.

Before they could alter course, they were in the middle of it. Now the leadsman chant changed from a lullaby to a sharp staccato cry. Twenty fathoms, ten fathoms, fifteen fathoms. The bottom was as irregular as a landscape in Scotland. Any moment the chant could go from twelve fathoms to none.

But the wind. Where was it? One moment the ship's sails

were full. The next they were limp, flapping in a weird calm. There was, Captain Jones estimated at a glance, a two-knot tide running in the water around them. God knows where it could shove the *Mayflower*, without wind enough to make headway. In all his years at sea, Christopher Jones had never been in a tighter box. The mates were taut with tension, the crew aghast. If this was Tucker's Terror, now they knew why that old salt was scared.

The passengers immediately sensed the crew's fears. After all those agonizing weeks, were they going to smash here, within sight of the promised land? By now the light was fading from the autumn sky. Anchoring for the night was a possibility. But when the tide ran out, they had no idea how close the bottom might be. A sudden storm, or even a mild swell, could be enough to smash the ship to pieces on the sands.

Once more all eyes turned to Christopher Jones. And once more he chose the bold decision. Run for the open sea, while there was still daylight to sail by. They might hit worse shoals before they were clear. But with luck, they would be safe before darkness fell. But only if they had wind. For some twenty minutes, none seemed to be forthcoming, and they wallowed helplessly in the breakers. Then, as if by conquering the Atlantic they had made her their slave, the ocean heaved an obedient sigh, and they were moving again. The helm was put over, and the ship came around through the crashing water. The leadsman went to work again, feeling his way through the breakers for the exit to the depths.

Another twenty minutes of anxious listening to the calls

of the sinking line and they began to hear the delightful numbers: "Forty fathoms at bottom, fifty fathoms at bottom." Safe, in enough water to float six *Mayflowers* stacked on top of one another. The dying sun threw huge red-streaked shadows over the sea as the ship emerged from the shoals that later generations would call Pollock's Rip. In a superb demonstration of seamanship, Captain Jones had conned her to safety without even a scratch on her hull.

But now another conference was in order. If the uncharted coast contained any more water like Tucker's Terror, they might be weeks reaching Hudson's River. Their maps told them nothing. They could not even trust them for distance. What looked like ten leagues might be a hundred. Maybe it would be wiser to settle here, on the New England coast, and waste no more of these precious days on the edge of winter.

Far into the night the leaders from Leyden and the leaders from London debated the situation, and finally decided to risk New England. In some ways the advantages, certain religious freedom and present proximity, outweighed the disadvantages, the lack of a patent and the supposedly severe winters. According to second mate Robert Coppin, who had sailed this coast in 1619, there was a fine harbor on the other side of Cape Cod, where they could safely anchor and explore the country.

They communicated their decision to Captain Jones the next morning, and he promptly brought the *Mayflower* about once more and began beating back up the coast. For him, making a landfall was simple enough. But for his passengers, the choice suddenly presented an alarming threat.

When the leaders announced that they had with due consideration decided to settle in New England rather than at Hudson's River, a shiver of mutinous fever ran through the ship.

The younger men—the bonded servants and those hired under contract—and some of the Londoners who, like Christopher Martin, felt they were being condemned to servitude by the changed terms of their contract with the London merchants, greeted the news of a New England landing as a call to revolution. These sober saints with their patent no longer had any right to control them. It was exactly the same situation Stephen Hopkins had experienced when shipwrecked in Bermuda in 1609. Landing on a shore where they had no right to go, the mutineers felt that they were automatically "freed from the government of any man." Edward Dotey and Edward Leister, who had listened attentively to their master's retelling of the Bermuda story on the voyage over, were among the loudest in their declarations of independence.

This was a genuinely alarming development. They needed every able-bodied man if they were going to get shelter up before the snow began to fall. Moreover, the servants and single men who were most likely to be affected by such thinking outnumbered the responsible family men who were depending on their muscle. The possibility of an armed revolt, bloodshed, murder, was by no means remote. In Bermuda, three of the mutineers had been hanged, and similar dissensions had come close to destroying Jamestown more than once over the last years.

All during the next day, November 10, the leaders of the

little expedition discussed the problem in the *Mayflower's* Great Cabin. Instinctively they shied away from any use of force—although Miles Standish may have growled that he was sure he could handle any resistance. Pastor Robinson had told them in his farewell letter that they were to become a "body politic." Why not become one now, in a formal and definite way, and thus cut the ground from beneath the rebels' arguments?

They had a model in the covenant which all the members of the Church of Leyden had signed and lived by for over a decade. William Brewster, as the university man among them, and Stephen Hopkins, also well educated, were probably given the assignment to draw up a brief "compact." While the *Mayflower* crept cautiously around the tip of Cape Cod, the two men went to work and soon had the wanted words on paper.

IN THE NAME OF GOD, AMEN

We whose names are underwritten, the loyal subjects of our dread Sovereign Lord King James by the Grace of God of Great Britain, France, Ireland, King, Defender of the Faith, etc.

Having undertaken, for the Glory of God and advancement of the Christian Faith and Honour of our King and Country, a voyage to plant the First Colony in the Northern Parts of Virginia, do by these presents solemnly and mutually in the presence of God and one of another, covenant and Combine ourselves together into a Civil Body Politic, for our better ordering and preservation and furtherance of the ends aforesaid, and by virtue hereof to enact, constitute and frame such just and equal laws, ordinances, Acts, Constitutions and Offices from time to time, as shall be thought most meet and convenient for the general good of the Colony, unto which we promise all due submission and obedience. In witness whereof we have hereunder subscribed our names at Cape Cod, the 11th of November, in the year of the reign of our Sovereign Lord King James of England, France and Ireland the eighteenth, and of Scotland the fifty-fourth. Anno Domini 1620.

The compact drawn, the leaders spent a restless night while the *Mayflower* "reached" back and forth off the tip of the Cape waiting for daylight. As dawn broke on the eleventh, they saw before them the wide harbor, now called Provincetown, almost encircled by the long, sandy fingers of the Cape. The leadsman chanted the fathoms, and the ship began the tricky business of entering. Meanwhile belowdeck, the passengers were assembled, and the leaders told them about the agreement they had drawn up. They wanted it signed before the anchor went down and any of the would-be mutineers openly revolted.

First came those who were entitled to the term Master. One by one they stepped up to an improvised table and signed. John Carver was first. He was followed by William Bradford, Edward Winslow, William Brewster, Isaac Allerton, Miles Standish, Samuel Fuller, William White. Then the leaders of the London group—Christopher Martin, William Mullins, Richard Warren, Stephen Hopkins.

Then the goodmen were invited to sign. This was the next social rank below master. Twenty-seven did so. Finally, four servants, including the obstreperous Edward Dotey and Edward Leister, signed on stern orders from their masters. A total of forty-one of the sixty-five males aboard signed. Thirteen of those who did not sign were sons of signers; their fathers' signatures covered their allegiance. Only nine servants and two of the hired sailors were omitted, probably because they were ill.

There was no consciousness of an historic occasion. They were not aware that they were signing a document in which historians would find foreshadowings of such sonorous phrases as "all men are created equal" and "government by the consent of the governed." On deck, while they signed, there came the chant of the leadsman, the bellowed orders of boatswain and mates as the ship advanced into the harbor. In a few hours they would be marching into a wilderness. This "compact" was simply another precaution against disaster.

One more piece of business remained—the election of a governor. John Carver was chosen to serve for one year. There was no opposition. The compact had been a masterful solution to the threatened revolt. Cowed and quiet, the speechmakers of the day before trooped above for a look at the New World.

From the crowded decks, the passengers gazed out at long, white sandhills that reminded them of the dunes of Holland, and on the other side, bristling forests that marched to the water's edge. "Instinctively many fell upon their knees," William Bradford says, "and blessed the God of Heaven who had brought them over the vast and furious ocean and delivered them from all the perils and miseries thereof, to set their feet on the firm and stable earth, their proper element."

At ten o'clock, after circling the harbor and finding numerous sandbars, Captain Jones prudently dropped his anchor about a mile from shore. The crew still had work to do. But Christopher Jones retired to his cabin for some much-needed rest. Since the lead had touched bottom at eighty fathoms, fifty-two hours earlier, he had not closed his eyes. Now he had his reward. The mates and boatswain took over, cursing the men aloft to furl the sails and secure the ship for port.

The passengers roamed from port to starboard, from stern to stem, studying the land before them. The longer they looked, the less elated they became. William Bradford, in a moment of deep feeling, explained why: "I cannot . . . but stand half amazed at this poor people's present condition. Being thus past the vast ocean, and a sea of troubles before in their preparation . . . they had now no friends to welcome them nor inns to entertain or refresh their weatherbeaten bodies, no houses or much less towns to repair to, to seek for succour. . . .

"Summer being done, all things stand upon them with a weatherbeaten face, and the whole country, full of woods and thickets, represented a wild and savage hue. If they looked behind them, there was the mighty ocean which they had passed and was now as a main bar and gulf to separate them from all the civil parts of the world. . . . Let it also be considered what weak hopes of supply and succour they left behind them. What could now sustain them but the Spirit of God and His grace?"

Chapter 8

THE PROMISED LAND

The young men, less daunted by the look of the wintry land, were frantic to go ashore. The ship's firewood was exhausted, and this was another reason for a combination work and exploring party. Sixteen men, armed with muskets and axes, piled into the *Mayflower's* longboat. Sandbars prevented them from landing on the beach. They had to wade ashore through three feet of water, not the most pleasant experience in early November. But the exultation of touching the solid earth once more was so great that no one minded a temporary chill.

Marching inland, they found that this tip of Cape Cod was a small neck of land, with the bay on one side and the ocean on the other. Beneath the sand was "excellent black earth." In the woods the countrymen among them spotted oaks, pines, sassafras, juniper, birch, holly, some ash and walnut. The forest was for the most part open, with few thickets or other underbrush except vines. But they found no fresh water, which discouraged thoughts of founding a colony here. Nor was there a sign of any "savage barbarians," as they called the Indians.

The explorers spent the afternoon cutting juniper, and at nightfall returned to the ship with a handsome load of this sweet-smelling wood. Soon the *Mayflower's* lower decks were rich with wilderness incense, and they all enjoyed their first hot meal in weeks.

The next day was Sunday, but anxious as they were to get on with the business of landing, the voyagers refused to violate their Sabbath. They spent the day in prayer and meditation, singing psalms and listening to a heartening sermon by William Brewster. For them, the presence of God was as important in this wilderness as the farms and houses they must create.

Captain Jones and his crew were less impressed with divinity, and this loss of a full day's work put some of them in a very bad temper. Jones urgently pointed out that supplies were running low and that he had a responsibility to his mates and crew as well as to his passengers. It was a long voyage home, and the longer they dawdled here, the less there would be to eat for everyone. He had no intention of landing in London with a crew of skeletons, and was going to keep enough food aboard to feed his men well on the way back, no matter how little this left the settlers on shore. There is no evidence that Jones was nasty about the need for haste—but some of his sailors were heard to mutter that they ought to dump these psalmsingers and their furniture and food on shore and haul sail on the spot.

The next day, Monday, November 13, everyone was up

early, and the divided shallop was hoisted out of the *May-flower's* hold and lowered into the longboat. Sailors and servants lugged her four parts through the shallow water to the beach, and the ship's carpenter looked her over. He did not like what he saw. The boat's seams had been opened by people sleeping in her on the gun deck, and it would take several days, perhaps two weeks, to put her back together and caulk her until she was watertight.

This was disheartening news. They were depending on the twenty-three-foot boat with her sail and oars to explore the coast quickly. While the men brooded over this problem, the women and children who had followed them ashore went to work on the accumulated laundry of their ten-week voyage. It was a long day's washing, and when it was finished, and the clothes hung on the *Mayflower's* rails and rigging to dry, the old ship must have looked like something out of fairyland.

For the children, the day ashore was a superb adventure. They raced wildly after the tremendous flocks of gulls feeding along the shore, dug clams and mussels out of the sand-flats as the tide ran out, and screamed with excitement when a school of whales surfaced in the bay, spouting and lolling in the sunny water.

Captain Jones and his sailors were as goggle-eyed by the whales as everyone else. They groaned with frustration at not having brought along any equipment to catch them. The master and his mates told the passengers that they could have made fifteen to twenty thousand dollars in a week without moving out of the harbor, and vowed it was better whale fishing than Greenland.

One leviathan eased his mighty bulk to within half a musket shot of the *Mayflower,* and lay there, dozing in the noon sunshine. Two of the sailors decided to give him a broadside and send him on his way. Hastily charging their muskets, they took aim, but when the first man pulled the trigger, his cranky gun blew up in his face. Miraculously, neither he nor those who were standing around him on deck watching the show were hurt by the flying fragments. As for the whale, he did not even stir. Finally, when he had his nap and was ready to leave on his own terms, he "gave a snuff, and away!"

Those who went ashore that day brought back baskets full of mussels, and many of the passengers and crew, willing to eat anything after their weeks of salt meat and biscuits, gulped them down greedily. Later that night, and most of the next day, they regretted it. As many another would-be gourmet has since discovered, the internal reaction was violent, and a good half the ship's company was laid low. But it was only a temporary fright and by Wednesday everyone was well again.

By this time the more adventurous among the men were for exploring the country on foot. It would be madness to wait for the shallop when there was a good chance of finding a site within walking distance. As they came into the harbor on Saturday morning, several keen-eyed observers had noticed what seemed to be a river running into the sea five or six miles down the shore. Since a navigable river was considered an essential part of the colony—ships could use it for loading and unloading—this might well be the place they wanted.

Governor Carver, however, was hesitant to risk precious manpower in such an exploration. To his eyes, the wintry forest had a hostile, implacable look. Without the shallop, a small party could be cut off and decimated by attacking savages. There was considerable argument back and forth, and finally Carver was persuaded.

"The willingness of the persons was liked," William Bradford says, "but the time itself, in regard of the danger, was rather permitted than approved." With a vast amount of cautious instructions and directions, Carver assigned sixteen men to go ashore under the command of Miles Standish. For "council and advice" to the hotblooded soldier, Carver assigned William Bradford, Stephen Hopkins, and Edward Tilley, another dependable member of the London group. Each man was equipped with helmet, musket, sword, and steel "corslet" or breastplate. Except for Standish, not a man had had any professional military experience. But the days that the captain had spent drilling them on board ship had not been wasted. They handled their long, clumsy guns with a fair degree of confidence.

The sailors rowed the explorers ashore, and they set out down the beach in single file, with Standish at their head. After they had marched about a mile, they saw five or six people with a dog coming toward them. At first they thought it was Captain Jones and his sailors who had gone ashore to do some hunting a few hours earlier. But the little clump of figures suddenly did an abrupt turn and vanished into the woods. Indians! The dog gamboled around the beach a while longer, while Standish urged his file to double time. But as they drew closer, a sharp whistle came from the woods, and the dog raced obediently after his savage masters.

Standish immediately demonstrated his pugnacity by ordering a vigorous pursuit of the savages. If there were more Indians in the woods, it would be fatal to let them get between them and the ship. But the red men ran away "with might and main." Foolishly now, the white men followed them. If the Indians were planning an ambush, they had made-to-order victims in these sixteen amateur woodsmen.

But the natives were as anxious to escape as the explorers were to catch them. They followed their "footings" for some ten miles, even tracking them up a hill, where the red men had paused to check on their pursuers. Darkness fell, with Standish and his men still far in the rear, and they made camp, kindled a fire, and posted three sentries for the night.

The next morning they again took up the Indians' trail. It was easy to be a scout in the sandy earth of the Cape. But after a few hours, they lost the track at the head of a long creek. Circling it, they picked it up again at the entrance of another stretch of woods. But this forest was by no means as open as the woods around the *Mayflower's* harbor. "We marched through boughs and bushes, and under hills and valleys, which tore our very armour in pieces," Bradford says. But the Indians had vanished, and by ten o'clock the exploring party was in deep trouble. They had had nothing to drink but a few swigs of brandy someone had thoughtfully stuffed in his pack. For food they had dined on biscuits and cheese, and now they were gasping for water.

With their tongues thick and lips dry, they fought their way out of the woods and found themselves in a "deep valley, full of brush, bayberry and long grass." A number of little paths or "tracts" ran through it. Wandering in a rough semicircle, they had stumbled into what is now called East Harbour in the town of Truro. While they surveyed the peaceful, windblown scene, a deer gamboled past. Then came the welcome cry: "Water!"

Water it was, and fresh, the first they had tasted since they boarded the *Mayflower*. "We were heartily glad," William Bradford says, "and sat us down and drank our first New England water with as much delight as ever we drank drink in all our lives."

Refreshed, they marched south to the waters of the bay, where they built a fire so the worried watchers on the *Mayflower* could locate them once more. Then they swung off down the beach in the direction of this "supposed river." Wherever they saw a break in the woods or a lay of land that had an interesting look, they investigated. Thus in a few more miles, they found themselves looking down on a "fine clear pond of fresh water" which is now Pond Village in Truro. Around this pleasant spot grew many small vines, and they saw several deer darting through the woods. The pond waters were thick with wild fowl.

Nearby they found about fifty acres of what was obviously cleared ground "fit for the plow." There were signs that this was an Indian farm. But once more the Indians remained invisible. The explorers went back to the beach and tramped for a few more hours. Soon Standish's single file was stretched out for the better part of a mile. He called a halt to wait for the stragglers to come up. Tramping through soft sand burdened with armor and heavy muskets was hard work.

They now abandoned the beach and struck into the woods again, following a little path to "certain heaps of sands." One heap was covered with old mats and had a wooden arch over it. In a little hole at the end was an earthen pot. Poking into it with their swords, they dug up a bow and several arrows, which crumbled in their hands. They decided they had stumbled on a graveyard, and dug no more. "We thought," Bradford says, "it would be odious unto them to ransack their sepulchres."

Not far away on this same woodland path they found the stubble of a harvested cornfield, strawberry and grape vines, and a "great store" of walnut trees full of nuts. They marched on and came upon two more well-gleaned cornfields, and then a place where "a house" had been, and four or five old planks laid together. Nearby was a "great kettle" obviously from a European ship. They stood for a moment around the desolate scene wondering if they were seeing the relics of some shipwrecked seamen who had tried to winter here and had succumbed to either cold or savages.

Then someone noticed another heap of sand at the top of a rounded hill nearby. They struggled up the steep slope and saw that whatever was under this mound was freshly buried. They could see how the sand had been smoothed by human hands not long before. Standish ordered thirteen of the men to stand in a ring, with their muskets ready, and told three others to start digging. They went to work with their swords and soon uncovered a "little old basket" full of corn. Excited, they dug further, and found another huge basket, full of "very fair corn of this year . . . some 36 goodly ears of corn, some yellow and some red and others mixed with blue."

It was, as Bradford says, "a very goodly sight." They had brought along seeds of wheat and barley, but they knew from English experience in Virginia that the crop that grew best in the New World was this corn, and one of the reasons they had been pursuing the Indians was to borrow or buy some.

All told, the basket held about four bushels of corn. What to do with it? For them, it was—or could be—more precious than gold. But they hesitated to begin their sojourn in the country by robbing the natives. "After much consultation," Bradford says, "we concluded to take the kettle and as much of the corn as we could carry away with us. And when our shallop came, if we could find any of the people, and come to parley with them, we could give them the kettle again, and satisfy them for the corn."

They took all thirty-six of the ears in the little basket, filled the kettle with loose corn, and hung it on a staff so that two men could carry it. Those who had room stuffed more in their pockets. The rest they buried, wishing they were not "so laden with armour" that they could not take more.

From the top of this rise, still known as Corn Hill, the explorers had a fine view of the surrounding country. They saw a small river to the south, which seemed to be part of the "opening" they had come to inspect. Marching on, they passed the ruins of an old fort or palisado—another unpleasant reminder of visits by earlier explorers. Reaching the river, they found that it was cut in half by a high bank at the mouth. This was the Pamet River, divided by "Old

Tom's Hill." The southern arm looked "not unlikely to be a harbour for ships," but whether it was salt or fresh, they had no time to investigate.

Governor Carver had given them strict orders to remain out no more than two days, and to check the river for fresh water would have required a march of several miles inland. They decided to leave that job to the shallop. But they did take time to investigate two canoes, one on either side of the river. "We could not believe it was a canoe until we came near it," Bradford says, communicating in this brief sentence the eerie feeling the explorers were beginning to have that this country was anything but deserted. Two canoes, one on either side of the river, was the way intelligent people might create a ferry service for those who wanted to cross. But where were these citizens of the forest?

With wary eyes and uncertain nerves, the scouting party tramped back to the fresh-water pond and made camp for another night. This time they put up a "barricado" of logs, stakes, and boughs to the windward, so that no one could creep up on them. Once more they were under the impression that they could easily outwit these savages at woodcraft. They kept "good watch," with three sentinels taking turns all night and with five or six inches of match cord glowing at all times.

The weather turned foul, raining and blowing furiously. By morning everyone was soaked, chilled, and discouraged. Worse, their powder and fuses were wet, and their usable muskets were reduced to a handful. To speed their pace, they decided to sink the kettle in the pond, and skirting the wood where they had almost had their armor ripped to pieces, they promptly got lost. "We were shrewdly puzzled," Bradford says.

Wandering through the woods, they came to a sapling that bowed down until it formed an archway over the path. They noticed a bow in the center of the archway and some acorns scattered around it. The leaders of the file were about to march right across these when Stephen Hopkins called out a warning. In his trip to Virginia, eleven years before, he had learned enough to recognize an Indian deer trap when he saw one.

Everyone gathered around, and Hopkins began telling them how the trap worked. William Bradford, who had been bringing up the rear and did not hear Hopkins' first warning, came strolling into the circle and inadvertently gave everyone a demonstration. Bradford stepped into the center of the trap and instantly the sapling sprang straight up in the air, and the poor fellow found himself dangling head down by one leg. If there had been no one around to help him, he might have been in serious trouble. "It was a very pretty device," he says, "made with a rope of their own making, and having a noose as artificially [cunningly] made as any roper in England can make and as like ours as can be."

After more wandering, they fumbled their way out of the woods and found themselves barred by East Harbour Creek. They were consoled by seeing three fine bucks plunging through the grass within musket shot. But they were gone before they could light their matchlocks. "We had rather have had one of them," Bradford says ruefully.

They also flushed some partridges along the creek bank

and roused great flocks of geese and ducks, which were "very fearful" and took off with an enormous clatter. The explorers were learning the hard way that if they were going to live off this country, they would have to acquire some stealth.

After more marching through woods and over sand and wading two tidal creeks, they trudged wearily onto the beach that is now called Long Point and fired off a musket to attract the *Mayflower,* a mile out in the harbor. Soon there were dozens of people running down the beach to greet them. Governor Carver and Captain Jones were ashore, along with many others, and the heroes received a tumultuous welcome. They had been gone almost three full days, and those who had been left behind had been alarmed when they failed to appear within the stated two-day period.

That night was an exciting time for passengers and crew as everyone listened to the explorers' descriptions of the country, the signs and glimpses of the Indians, the game, the soil, the rivers and woods. But the corn was the biggest excitement. The ex-farmers among them, such as William Bradford, were stirred by the size of the kernels, which meant rich soil and good harvests to come.

William Bradford saw a parallel with the Israelites entering the Promised Land. They too had sent sixteen men exploring, under the command of a brave captain, and had brought back "the fruit of the land" for their brethren to see. The comparison was startling, and Bradford says his friends were "marvelously glad and their hearts encouraged."

The corn was carefully stored aboard the ship "for seed,"

and for the next few days, every effort was made to repair the shallop. When that proved slow work, the passengers decided it might be faster to build a new one. There was much "seeking out wood and helving of tools and sawing of timber," Bradford tells us. But the geography of their harbor was a fatal hindrance to the project. They could only land in the heavy longboat at high water, and even then they had to wade ashore, "oftentimes . . . to the middle of the thigh, and oft to the knees." The weather also failed to cooperate. It turned cold and stormy, and soon everyone who was in the habit of going ashore ("some did it necessarily and some for their own pleasure," Bradford says) were down with coughs and colds.

This attempt to build a boat by men who had never built one before was a sign of their growing desperation. The hollow cheeks and weary faces of their women and children, growing steadily weaker on the stale ship's food, haunted them. But they could do nothing but endure until November 27, when the carpenter finally announced that the shallop was ready to sail. Instantly another obstacle loomed. The four men they had hired to sail the shallop were sick. How could amateurs handle this big, unwieldy boat with its cumbersome sail? Once again they had to take their problem to Christopher Jones. The captain generously agreed to lend them ten of his seamen to man the shallop—and offered to take command of her himself.

Chapter 9

Cold harbor

Twenty-four men, armed and armored as before and under Miles Standish's command, boarded the shallop and the longboat. Those in the longboat were to go ashore and march down the beach to the mouth of the Pamet River, where the shallop would rendezvous with them and carry all hands up the river for exploration. In an unprecedented move, the passengers made Captain Jones the expedition leader. "We thought it best herein," Bradford says, "to gratify his kindness and forwardness." Bradford was once more among the marchers, and this time he was joined by his good friend Edward Winslow.

Winter was on them now, fastening deadly fingers of ice on their flesh. Snow flurries howled across the bay as they shoved off from the *Mayflower*. "Rough weather and cross winds" were so severe that both the longboat and the shallop had to run for the nearest beach, where everyone waded ashore in water above the knees. Jones surveyed the churning bay and declared that any further progress in the shallop was out of the question.

Bradford, Winslow, and the younger men who were going to march to the river on foot anyway decided to push on for another six or seven miles. That night it froze, and the snow continued to lash them. No clothing they had brought from Holland prepared them for this kind of exposure. Holland winters were cold, but all these men had worked in houses and shops. Huddled in their worn cloaks, some, in William Bradford's somber phrase, "took the original of their death here."

At eleven o'clock the next morning, the shallop arrived to pick up the chilled, coughing campers. With a good if biting wind, they sailed briskly down to the mouth of the Pamet River. They were now with a man who, like all sailors, had the instincts of an explorer. As they approached the river's mouth, Captain Jones suggested they give the place a name. In a wry testimony to the weather, the explorers decided to call it Cold Harbor.

Once more the marching party debarked at the hill between the two creeks, and slogged along through six-inch snow while the shallop sailed beside them. Sounding revealed twelve feet of water in the river at high tide—not enough for ships, but deep enough to handle good-sized boats such as the shallop. They covered five miles before dusk began to darken the sky.

Captain Jones, who had been marching on foot all the way, confessed he was weary and suggested they make camp. They settled under the bows of some pine trees and sent out hunters who came back with three fat geese and six ducks. William Bradford says they ate them "with soldiers stomachs." Except for a few nibbles of cheese and biscuits, it was the first food they had had all day.

They had planned to march to the head of the Pamet River where they hoped to find fresh water. But in the morning, they conferred and found many objecting to the poor soil in the vicinity and to the lack of a protected harbor for shipping. What good was fresh water if they lacked soil to grow their food and a harbor to trade with visitors? The dissenters carried the day, and they decided to retrace their steps.

It was very discouraging. Snow on the ground and two full days wasted on this exploration. They had to find a place soon or face total disaster. To make themselves and the others feel that the trip was not a complete waste of time, they decided to cross over to the other branch of the river and dig up the corn they had left behind. On the riverbank they found another ghostly evidence of their invisible hosts—a canoe lay on the dry ground. Out in the river were a flock of geese, and the explorers showed they were learning the hunter's art by killing a couple with a single shot.

They picked up the geese in the canoe and then used it to ferry themselves across the river, seven or eight at a time. Down the other side of the little stream they trudged and up the steep slope of Corn Hill. There they went to work with their swords once more. But the ground was so frozen that they could not get more than a foot below the surface, and even this amount of earth they had to "wrest up with levers." It was another alarming proof of winter's tightening hand.

But the digging was good. They found the corn that they had left behind and, in a place nearby, a bottle of oil. Not far away they found more corn and a bag of beans. Altogether they now had ten bushels, more than enough for seed. They consoled their consciences by again resolving to make restitution to the people they were robbing as soon as they could get in communication with them. Then they fell to marveling about how providential it was that they had made their first exploration on foot. Now, with the ground covered with snow, it would have been impossible to spot the telltale fresh earth where the corn had been buried.

Toward nightfall the sky began to look gloomy, and the wind had a damp, snowy taste. Captain Jones had had enough of exploring and was anxious to get back to his cabin aboard the *Mayflower*. A number of others were worn out and feverish from the brutal weather, but the younger men, haunted by those wan faces aboard the ship, refused to quit so soon. They sent Jones back with the corn and the sick, and eighteen camped on the beach for the night. They told the shallop to return the next day, bringing mattocks and spades so they could do some real digging.

The next morning they followed "beaten paths and tracks" of the Indians into the woods, hoping one of them would lead "to some town or houses." It was not only the matter of paying for the corn. These red men knew the country. They could tell them about good harbors, fresh-water rivers, lakes that lurked invisibly behind these frozen hills and barren trees. Suddenly the twisting trails converged upon "a very broad beaten path" almost two feet wide. They must be close to a village! Quickly they lit their matches and prepared to defend themselves if necessary, but after another half hour of trudging they realized it was only a path down which Indians drove deer when they were hunting.

They wasted the morning on this wandering, covering about twelve miles without finding a sign of a living man or woman. They came back to the beach by another route, and as they emerged into the "plain ground" they saw a long, low mound resembling a grave. It was also covered with boards which made them think it might be more corn. At any rate they promptly started to dig.

They found first a mat, under that a bow in good condition, and under that another mat and then a board about three-quarters of a yard long and finely carved and painted with prongs on the top like a crown. Between the mats there were bowls, trays, dishes, and other trinkets. Next was another mat and finally two bundles, one large, one small. Opening the larger one they found a quantity of fine red powder and the bones and skull of a man. There was also a knife, a packing needle, and "two or three old iron things," all bound up in a sailor's canvas blouse and cloth britches. The red powder seemed to be a kind of embalming agent; it had a strong but not unpleasant smell and was as fine as any flour.

In the second bundle they found more of the same powder and the bones and head of a small child. About the legs and the other parts of the withered body were bound strings and bracelets of what the explorers called "fine white beads." They would soon learn to recognize these beads as wampum, Indian currency. But the real mystery in these two graves grew from the skull of the man—a fine shock of blond hair. Some wondered if it were an Indian lord or king, but Stephen Hopkins and others who knew more about the natives vowed that no one had ever seen an Indian with brown, much less yellow hair. Others thought it was the grave of a Christian man and child—perhaps a lord on the way to Virginia with his son, shipwrecked here and buried with honors by the awed natives. But several others looked around them at the silent land with nervous shivers and wondered if they were not looking on the victims of a savage slaughter.

Meanwhile the shallop arrived from the *Mayflower*, and, armed with mattocks and spades, they began wandering through the woods in search of more likely places to dig. Two of the sailors joined them and soon proved they had sharper eyes than the settlers. They spotted two Indian houses hidden in the trees. The explorers had walked within a hundred yards of them without noticing them.

Their muskets at ready, the two salts had ventured inside and, finding both places empty, invited the rest of the party to join them. The houses were made from long, young sapling trees, with both ends stuck in the ground. They were rounded on top, somewhat like an igloo, and covered down to the ground with "thick and well-wrought mats." The door was not over a yard high and was covered by another mat, but inside there was room enough to stand. In the center there were four little stakes knocked into the ground and small sticks laid over these. Here the residents did their primitive cooking; the smoke went out through a small hole in the top. Around the fire were more mats where the inhabitants slept and lounged.

The visitors were fascinated to find wooden bowls and trays, dishes, earthen pots, and hand baskets made of crab shells. There was also an English pail lacking a handle, and many different kinds of baskets, some with interesting black and white patterns on them. On the walls were hung three deer heads, one fresh killed, as well as an astonishing number of deer feet and eagles' claws. Finally there were two or three baskets full of parched acorns, pieces of fish, and a piece of broiled herring.

Obviously, the inhabitants had not been gone long. They might be somewhere in the silent forest now, watching. The empty houses seemed another even more positive sign of sullen hostility. Perhaps this was why the visitors felt free to take "some of the best things" with them. Once more they promised each other they would make restitution. In fact there were some beads and other trinkets in the shallop which they would bring back immediately as proof that they were not stealing but only wanted to trade.

But then the sailors were bellowing from the shore that the tide was running out fast and if they did not hurry, they would never launch the shallop and would all end up spending another night on the freezing beach. Forgetting about the beads, they seized their loot and hurried down to help shove the heavy boat into the deep water.

Back at the *Mayflower* they found both good and bad news. Susanna White had given birth to a son, a healthy boy whom the parents decided to call Peregrine. The rest of the ship's company was not so healthy. Everyone was wracked with coughs, wearier than ever, if possible, with the awful food and almost pathologically anxious to get off their wooden prison and walk in freedom on the earth once more.

William Bradford was particularly disturbed by his wife Dorothy's drawn face and harried eyes. The sweet and smiling girl he had loved in Holland seemed to have been replaced by a listless, sulky woman who barely responded to his questions and caresses. There was no psychiatric language in 1620; the word "depression" had not yet been invented. Worse, William Bradford had little time to give Dorothy the help she so desperately needed. More and more, during the two exploring expeditions, the men had turned instinctively to him for leadership in the dozens of small decisions. Inevitably now he played a dominant role in the violent discussion that engulfed the *Mayflower's* passengers and radically threatened the precarious harmony they had thus far maintained.

Some were for settling right where they were. There was ground already cleared for corn, and they had seen its rich fruits. The harbor was convenient enough. They had no wish to set up a rival to London Port, did they? A landing for fair-sized boats was all they needed. Third, the fishing out here on Cape Cod was superb. Whales had continued to gambol about the ship. They could make a fortune from the sea alone. Moreover, there were no swamps in the vicinity, and the hilly terrain made it easily defensible. But all these arguments were frills to the central urgency—the growing harshness of the weather, the deterioration of everyone's health, the dwindling food supply.

Others, led by Bradford, differed violently. They cried

that it would be folly to settle on a second-rate place when an ideal site might be only a few miles away. The decision, they pointed out, was irrevocable. They were going to build houses, a fort, the sort of things that could not be picked up and transported. Moreover the fresh water around Corn Hill was all in ponds. How did anyone know it might not dry up in the summer heat? If they settled on top of Corn Hill, every drop of water would have to be lugged up the steep slope.

There had to be better places along the coast than their newly named Cold Harbor. Several excited speakers urged a place called Anguum, some sixty miles to the north (probably present-day Ipswich). According to the sailors there was a good harbor for ships there, better soil and better fishing.

The settle-now party angrily demurred at such a trip. With the sudden storms of winter they might lose both men and boat, and that would ruin everything. Who could say how long such a trip might take in foul weather? They might be gone for weeks. They all had to get off this ship before they rotted away! Grimly underscoring their urgency, Edward Thompson, William White's young servant, died on December 4.

The death sobered both sides, and they agreed to compromise. Those who wanted further exploration would make one more trip, but it would be within the limits of the present bay. Anguum was absolutely ruled off limits. The explorers turned now to second mate Robert Coppin, the man who knew the coast best. Pointing to the bluff across the bay, now called Manomet, he said there was a navigable river and good harbor there, less than twenty-four miles away.

Last year Coppin and some sailors had gone ashore there and tried to trade with the Indians. They had offered them a harpoon, and one of the tricky savages had run off into the woods with it. Whereupon the disgusted sailors had named the place Thievish Harbor. The would-be explorers exultantly brought this news to Governor Carver. Peering nervously across the gray, wintry water, Carver wondered if even this was too far to risk the few healthy men left and the precious shallop. But he finally agreed, cautioning them that they were not to go a foot beyond the place.

The explorers nodded in grim and reluctant agreement. Those with foresight, such as William Bradford, knew that it was their last chance to find a place where they could hope to survive. But a last chance was better than no chance at all.

Chapter 10

A BATTALION OF DEMONS

The day before the explorers were to leave, the whole ship had a fright that redoubled their anxiety to get ashore. Crowded into the Great Cabin along with personal possessions were the weapons the men took ashore with them on the various expeditions and landings. To save steps, they had moved a small barrel of powder into the cabin. It was now half full. Into this explosive situation crept fourteen-year-old Francis Billington to play Bold Hunter.

Standing within four feet of the open barrel of gunpowder, he proceeded to prime a handy musket, and pull the trigger. The muskets of 1620 emitted a tremendous flash from the powder in the firing pan. If a single spark had leaped into the barrel of gunpowder, the *Mayflower* would have become an instantaneous shambles. Several people were standing about the cabin at the time, yet they, too, were unharmed by the flash. The shaken passengers saw it as a miracle of God's mercy.

The explorers had planned to leave on Tuesday, December 5, the same day that Francis Billington almost blew them up. The weather was too foul. Wednesday's weather was not much better, but they decided they could not waste another day. The numbers and the composition of the exploring party were in themselves ominous signs of deterioration. Only the leaders and the sturdiest young men were now willing to venture out on the winter sea. Miles Standish, John Carver, William Bradford, Edward Winslow, Edward and his brother John Tilley, and John Howland volunteered. From the London group came Richard Warren and Stephen Hopkins and his servant Edward Dotey. Two of the seamen they had hired to man their shallop were well enough to go, but Captain Jones was still feeling the effects of the last venture. However, the two mates, John Clark and Robert Coppin, volunteered along with the master gunner and three sailors.

Not even this handful of volunteers were all healthy. William Bradford says that as they beat about the harbor trying to get clear of the sandy point that enclosed it, two men were "very sick" and Edward Tilley fainted with the cold. The ship's gunner was also "sick unto death," but he stayed with them largely because he hoped that this time they would meet some Indians with whom he could trade trinkets for beaver skins.

It took them two hours of dreadful sailing to reach the shore of Cape Cod, where the northeast wind was less ferocious. Out on the open water it had come howling down on them, drenching boat and men in a freezing spray. "The water froze on our clothes and made them, many times, like coats of iron," Bradford says.

They sailed along the shore for about twenty miles but
"saw neither river nor creek." Finally they rounded a point
and found themselves in what is now called Wellfleet Bay.
For a moment they thought they had found their home.
There was more than enough shelter for good-sized ships
here, but night was coming on and there was no time to
explore the shoreline. They made for the nearest beach, and
as they drew close they saw "ten or twelve Indians very busy
about a black thing."

The red men became extremely agitated when they saw
the explorers and ran up and down as if they were carrying
something away, and finally vanished into the woods. Sandbars made landing difficult. The explorers finally worked
their way to shore five or six miles from the Indians. By now
it was dusk. It would be dangerous to follow the Indians in
the darkness. They made a "barricado, cut some fire wood
and set out sentinels." As they shivered around their fire
they suddenly saw another glow many miles down the wide
beach. It was the Indians, and all through the long night the
two campfires glowed while the darkness remained an im-
passable gulf between them.

In the morning, the beach was deserted. Once more the
Indians had vanished, leaving the white men alone on the
edge of the silent winter wilderness. They decided to divide
their group, eight men going in the shallop and twelve marching along the shore to explore what they hoped was their new
home. They were swiftly disappointed. "We found it only
to be a bay, without either river or creek coming into it,"
William Bradford says.

The land was level, but the soil was not especially fruitful. They did find two small streams of fresh water, the first they had seen. They also found one of the "black things" around which the Indians had been working. It was a "great fish" which the sailors called a grampus, about fifteen feet long, black on top and white in the belly. It was "fleshed like a swine" with about two inches of fat under its skin. The shallop found two others farther down the bay, also dead on the sands. The explorers studied them wistfully. There was valuable oil in their fat, if only they had the time and tools to extract it. Farther up the beach they found the grampus that the Indians had been cutting up. They had sliced strips about forty-five inches long and eight inches broad from the dead fish and carried them away to boil down for oil.

The explorers followed the Indians' tracks along the sand until they "struck into the woods" beside a large pond (Great Pond in Eastham). Someone thought they saw an Indian wigwam among the trees, and leaving the shallop out on the bay, the twelve landsmen marched into the woods. They found a path that led them to a clearing where corn had once been planted, but for some reason the ground had not been tilled that year.

Not far away they made an even more puzzling discovery. In a silent clearing stood a great, square fence made of young saplings four or five yards high, each planted two or three feet in the ground. Within the square was an immense grave-yard. Some graves were bigger than others; a few had small fences around them. One or two even had Indian wigwams built over them. Outside the main fence were other graves, not so sumptuous. Here surely was the site of some immense disaster. Hundreds of people were buried here. Not far away they found more corn ground, also untilled, and four or five wigwams, abandoned, with only two or three old mats and a little sedge hanging from them.

What was the explanation? The desolate winter woods seemed even more eerie to the baffled explorers as they exchanged bewildered glances. Was there nothing in this land but death? Where were the living people they had seen on the beach yesterday? "We went ranging up and down till the sun began to draw low," Bradford says. "All this while we saw no people."

They hurried out of the woods just before dark, and signaled the shallop, which was a long way off down the bay. The men in the boat were vastly relieved to see the party emerge from the woods. The sailors had expected them to stay on the beach, and when they vanished (it had been about ten o'clock when they turned into the woods) the alarm had been great.

After some waiting for the tide, the shallop made it ashore. The marchers were "both weary and faint." They had eaten nothing all day, but before they could dine they had to chop more wood for a barricade and for their fire. The work seemed more exhausting each time they did it. Their strength was ebbing fast.

Huddling once more around the campfire, they dined on "such victuals as we had"—the nauseating salt meat and iron biscuits. They then set out their sentinels and tried to get some sleep. About midnight, as the sentinels paced wearily up and down, beating their hands and stamping their feet against the cold, the woods suddenly erupted with "a great and hideous cry." A battalion of demons seemed to be rushing down on them. "Arm! Arm!" the sentries shouted. The sleepers scrambled wildly for their guns and rushed to their barricade. The howling chorus seemed to engulf them from all sides, but there was no attack. They shot off a couple of muskets, and the noise abruptly ceased. One of the sailors told of a similar experience when he had spent the night ashore in Newfoundland. The noisemakers, he assured them, were not men or demons but wolves.

Those who could went back to sleep until 5 A.M. By mutual agreement, in this first gray light, the camp began to stir. Two or three, still somewhat nervous about the previous night's uproar, fired off their muskets to make sure they were in working order. After morning prayer, they stoked their fire and prepared to make some breakfast.

While the food was heating, someone suggested they could begin to carry their things down to the shallop, several hundred yards away across the broad beach in the shallow water. Those who were still nervous thought "it was not best to carry the armour down." Others scoffed and said they would be all the readier to start once they got rid of their heavy iron corselets. Two or three others said they would carry their own armour when they went themselves. All told, sixteen of the twenty surrendered their guns and armour, and the working party lugged them down the beach to the shallop. There they discovered the tide was not high enough to launch the boat, and they piled the guns and armour by the water's edge and came back to breakfast. It was an almost fatal mistake. The weeks of wandering through the deserted woods had made even Captain Standish somewhat careless.

Suddenly, as they sat down to breakfast, the woods erupted with the same awful cry that had shaken them at midnight. "We knew [them] to be the same voices," Bradford says, "though they varied their notes." Wolves howling again at dawn? The explorers exchanged uneasy glances. Then came another cry beneath the ear-shattering howl. "They are men Indians! Indians!" In the same instant a barrage of arrows came hissing out of the semidarkness to thud against the barricade, inches away from the horrified white men's heads.

The warning cry had come from one of the sentinels who had wandered into the woods while waiting for breakfast. He was no longer on duty but simply doing some idle exploring. Were it not for his morning constitutional, the whole group probably would have been slaughtered around the campfire.

They were still far from safe. The men who had left their guns and armour down by the shallop rushed out of the barricade and legged it across the broad beach for their weapons. The Indians came streaming out of the woods to cut them off. These savages were no fools; they had evidently been watching the white men all night and had chosen to attack the moment they had separated themselves from their weapons. But a few of those who had stacked their guns and armour had retained their swords, and they met the first shock of the Indian assault while the others went on to the muskets. The scuffle on the sand ended abruptly when two or three got their clumsy matchlocks going and fired. The savages fled back into the woods.

Meanwhile, those around the fire were still under fierce assault. Their barricade was a three-sided affair with an opening to leeward, and through this opening the wily red men poured clouds of arrows. Standish temporarily discouraged them with a single shot from his more modern snaphaunce. Another man fired into the trees immediately after the captain, but when William Bradford and a fourth marksman stepped to the opening, Standish ordered them to hold their fire.

It was too dark to see anything out there in the trees, and if the Indians tried a frontal assault they would need every bullet. The bloodcurdling whoops and howls continued to come from the woods. "Woach! Ha! Ha! Hach! Woach!" was how they sounded to William Bradford.

Through the din, those at the barricade shouted to those at the shallop: "How is it with you?"

"Well, well," they shouted back. "Be of good courage!"

"Give us fire. Give us fire," several other voices called. They needed a flame to light their matchlocks. One of the barricade defenders grabbed a log out of the fire and raced down the beach to them. Everyone was armed now, but split into two groups. The explorers' position was precarious. Those around the shallop hesitated to return to the barricade which looked more and more like a trap. They assumed that Standish and his three musketeers would fall back to the boat, but the sturdy captain declined to surrender the food and equipment around the campfire without a fight.

He rightly guessed that the Indians were awed by the white men's muskets, and now it was light enough to see their enemies flitting back and forth through the trees. Though the howls continued, the attack seemed to be dwindling. Only one man, obviously their leader, drew close enough to do any real damage. "A lusty man, no wit less valiant," Bradford says, "he stood behind a tree within half a musket shot of us and there let his arrows fly at us." The chief shot three arrows which were "all avoided," while the white men blasted at him with three musket shots at a range of about forty yards. Finally one man took full aim at him and "made the bark and splinters of the tree fly about his ears."

The chief gave "an extraordinary cry" and fled. His savage cohorts vanished with him like so much smoke. The shaken white men were left alone once more on the edge of the silent forest.

Miles Standish decided there was only one way to counter such aggression. Leaving six men to guard the shallop, he marched the other thirteen a quarter of a mile into the woods after their attackers. He drew them up in a rank, and they shouted defiantly several times and shot off a couple of muskets. Standish wanted the Indians to see they were neither afraid nor discouraged.

The exact number of their attackers was difficult for the explorers to determine. "We could not guess there were less than thirty or forty," William Bradford says, "though some thought that there were many more. Yet in the dark of the morning, we could not so well discern them among the trees." They collected eighteen of their arrows. They were well made, some headed with brass, others with horn, and others with eagles' claws. Miraculously, so it seemed to the explorers, not a man among them was touched, although "many being close by us and on every side of us and some coats which hung up in our barricado were shot through and through." Governor Carver suggested that they give thanks to God for their deliverance. They knelt on the sand and did so. Then after christening the beach "The First Encounter," a name it still possesses, they boarded the shallop and set sail for "Thievish Harbor" of Robert Coppin's description.

They continued to hug the coast hoping to find a closer river or bay, but they saw neither. Meanwhile the weather began to grow ugly, snow and rain mixing in a mounting wind. By midafternoon it was a roaring gale, and they were plunging through heavy seas. Now the beating that the shallop had taken in the *Mayflower's* gun deck began to tell. The hinges of the rudder suddenly broke, and two men had to steer with oars. "The seas were grown so great that we were much troubled and in great danger," William Bradford says.

Night began to fall over the angry water, making their situation even more precarious. Then Robert Coppin called out: "Be of good cheer! I see the harbor!" They began running before the furious northeast wind, with the sea leaping mountainously around them. A prudent captain would have shortened his sail, but they were desperate to make the harbor while there was still some light. Then came a wilder blast of wind, and with a sickening crack the mast split in three pieces and went overboard.

Furious work now in the dark foaming water. Men leaped at the remnants of the mast and clinging halyards to cut them free before the shallop wallowed into the trough and capsized. In sixty seconds of frantic hacking they cut everything away and seizing the oars pulled with all their dwindling strength for the harbor ahead.

They had a flood tide and the wind at their stern, and for a few minutes progress was good, but up in the bow Robert Coppin suddenly peered through the dusk and lost his head completely.

"Lord be merciful unto us," he cried. "I have never seen this place before." Through the gloom, Coppin saw a cove full of pounding breakers. Wildly he shouted to first mate John Clark to run her ashore there. Clark, equally rattled, was about to do so—a decision that could well have destroyed the shallop and drowned everyone.

But one of the *Mayflower* seamen who was steering with the other oar unexpectedly took command. "If you be men," he roared, "about with her or we are all cast away!" The men at the oars put their backs into it and brought the heavy boat around. Their new commander bade them be of good cheer and "row lustily," for he saw a "fair sound" before them where they could ride out the storm in safety. Groping along in total darkness now, the explorers did indeed soon find calmer water and next worked their way into the shelter of some kind of land.

They had no idea where they were. After their morning clash with the Indians, most were afraid to go ashore. Some were afraid they would freeze to death huddled there in the cold rain. Around midnight, the wind shifted to northwest and the temperature plunged even lower. "It froze hard," Bradford says.

This was too much for John Clark, who had regained his composure and announced that he was going ashore and build a fire. If there were Indians around, it was better to die quickly under a tomahawk stroke than freeze to death inch by inch out here on the water. A few men followed him and soon had a big blaze roaring on the beach. After watching for awhile from the pitching, ice-encased boat and seeing no war party leap out of the darkness, everyone decided it was the kind of a night that would keep even Indians at home and joined the *Mayflower's* courageous first mate around the fire.

Warmth was their only consolation that night. Everything else that had happened could only plunge them even further into desperate gloom. They had no idea where they were. This so-called Thievish Harbor of Robert Coppin's memory might not even exist. They knew now that the Indians were ferociously hostile. Everything seemed to point to dwindling chances of success and even survival.

But the next day they felt better. "God gave them a morning of comfort and refreshing," William Bradford says. They awoke to a clear, fair world full of brilliant winter sunshine. They found themselves to be on an island "secure from Indians, where they might dry their stuff, fix their pieces and rest themselves."

Robert Coppin, calmer now, declared it was indeed the Thievish Harbor of his memory. Entering last night in the gloom and storm, he had mistook the first headland, the Gurnet, for Saquish Head. They decided to name the island after John Clark in gratitude for his courage in leading them to safety on it.

The view from the island was heartening after so many weeks of fruitless searching along the shore. Wooded hills, glistening with snow, formed a great amphitheater around the almost completely landlocked bay. The silence was broken only by the sea and a gull's occasional cry, giving the meditative explorers time to wonder and stare. Had they finally found their home?

The next day was Sunday and anxious as they were to explore the harbor, they once more refused to violate their Sabbath. They spent the day in prayer and meditation. The following morning, December 11, they were up at dawn. The weather continued to be sunny and mild. They had set a new mast in the shallop, and after a short sail across the quiet harbor they made their first landing in Plymouth.

William Bradford, the eyewitness historian of the day, neglects to tell us where. It may well have been upon the historic rock, which made a convenient landing place at half tide. This is the only possible resemblance to the traditional image of the occasion. There were no Indians to greet them. No women, no children by their sides, no *Mayflower* in the background. Only an empty harbor and a barren, silent land greeted this weather-beaten, bedraggled band of desperate men.

They formed up under Miles Standish's stern orders, lit their matches, and, with muskets ready, "marched onto the land." They liked what they saw. There were "diverse corn-fields and little running brooks," William Bradford says. "A place . . . fit for situation. At least it was the best they could find, and the season and their present necessity made them glad to accept of it."

We do not know whether they immediately christened the place. It would seem likely, since they had named many other sites they had discovered en route. But the confusion and hesitation which had marked their exploration hardly suggest that they possessed a copy of John Smith's map, on which the harbor was already called Plymouth. Later, they would tell visitors that they had named it Plymouth themselves, because "Plymouth in Old England was the last town they left in the native country; and for that they received many kindnesses from some Christians there."

For now, names were not important. It was the place itself, the promise of its soil, the protection of the ample harbor, that made their pulses beat. They were so anxious to bring the good news back to the *Mayflower*, they decided to sail straight across the twenty-five miles of open water to the tip of Cape Cod, rather than hug the coast as they had done on their outward voyage. It was a dangerous move in a small boat at that time of year. But for once the weather proved kind. They skimmed across the bay in brilliant sunshine and tied up alongside the *Mayflower* that afternoon.

Exclamations of joy, tears of relief greeted the explorers as they climbed aboard. They had been gone a full week, and many had given them up for lost. Young husbands, such as Edward Winslow, joyfully embraced their wives. William Bradford looked eagerly for Dorothy's smile, but she was not on deck. Then he noticed the uneasy eyes, the hesitant mouths of those closest to him. Perhaps then his old friend and foster father, William Brewster, stepped out of the crowd and took him by the arm. One look at his solemn face and Bradford knew the worst.

Mournfully, on the *Mayflower's* high poop, the man who had led William Bradford on this long voyage told him how his young wife had died. In some unknown way she had fallen overboard and drowned before anyone could come to her aid with a rope or spar. Though neither spoke it, both men almost certainly knew the dreaded word that lay between them. After six weeks of contemplating the melancholy winter face of the New World, Dorothy Bradford had lost her faith in her husband and her God and had killed herself.

William Bradford must have wept. Had his own carefully concealed doubts which had tempted him to leave his son behind destroyed the woman who trusted in his strength? A chorus of ifs and might have beens echoed in Bradford's numb mind. If young John had come with them, if Bradford himself had not been so preoccupied with his enthusiasm for exploring, his involvement in the decisions and debates on where to settle. . . .

We have no certain proof that Dorothy Bradford took her own life. But the strange circumstances of her death, and Bradford's total silence on the subject for the rest of his long life have raised the conjecture to near certainty in the minds of many Plymouth historians. It was a bitter homecoming for the young leader, and it would have broken many men. But William Bradford was not alone. His friends crowded around to comfort him. They had been inclined to lean on him. Now he needed help. It was the first of many moments when they would demonstrate the meaning of their covenant to love and cherish one another with the unhesitating charity urged by St. Paul.

Dorothy was not their only loss. The day the shallop sailed, little Jasper More, one of the three orphaned brothers whom Thomas Weston had hired out as servants to John Carver, died of the same combination of scurvy and pneumonia-like fever that had taken William Butten while at sea. The next day, James Chilton had died, leaving a grief-stricken wife and daughter to be cared for by the colony. A dozen others were prostrate in their bunks with the same sickness.

To a vigorous young man such as William Bradford, with natural gifts of leadership, it must have seemed vital for them to get the *Mayflower* to Plymouth harbor without losing another day. But Governor John Carver, older and less incisive, was anxious to give everyone a voice in the final decision. So they spent three more days in debate and deliberation before finally voting to settle in Plymouth. On December 15, the *Mayflower* weighed anchor and stood across the bay for their new home.

But Captain Jones, careful sailor that he was, did not at all like the looks of the narrow channel into Plymouth harbor and flatly refused to negotiate it under a northwest wind. They bore up and spent another night at sea. Cruising idly back and forth in the deep water, another debate broke out between those who favored Plymouth and those who still clung to the idea of settling at the tip of Cape Cod. It might take them days to work their way into this harbor, days they could not afford to waste. The Plymouth party was on the defensive and agreed that if serious difficulty developed the next day, they would consider a return to Cape Cod.

But in the morning, the wind came up fair and Captain Jones eased his old ship down the narrow channel and past the Gurnet and Saquish Head into the placid waters near Clark's Island. Within a half hour after they dropped anchor, the wind changed. Again many saw it as a sign of God's hand in helping them choose the place. William Bradford says, "If we had been leaded [hindered] but a little, we had gone back to Cape Cod."

The next day was Sunday, and once more the leaders from Leyden refused to violate their Sabbath, though they were doubly eager to explore this harbor. By now, Captain Jones and his sailors had become resigned to this aspect of their passengers. In fact, a small admiration had begun to creep among many of the crewmen. These people did not have the kind of wordy religion that they heard from country parsons back home. They lived their faith.

On Monday, Captain Jones, his explorer's instincts revived, volunteered to command the shallop for a trip ashore. Taking four of his sailors and a well-armed party of passengers under the command of Miles Standish, they marched seven or eight miles into the woods. They found neither Indians nor Indian corn, but there were cleared fields where corn had obviously once been planted. There were no navigable rivers, but four or five brooks with "very sweet, fresh water" ran into the harbor. They liked the looks of the soil, "excellent black mould," and trees for lumber were abundant. There were also sand and gravel and "excellent clay" for pots. All in all it was "a most hopeful place."

They spent the night aboard the *Mayflower* and the next morning went ashore again in the shallop for more exploring. This time they found "a very pleasant river and sailed up it for three miles." They named it after the *Mayflower's* captain, and it is stilled called Jones River today. At high tide a 30-ton ship could go up it, but at low tide even the shallop scraped bottom.

In spite of this, many people thought that it would be best to settle up the river. There would be less danger of attack by

French or Spanish privateers. Others thought it would be too far from fishing, which was to be their "principal profit," and surrounded as it was by woods, they would be in constant danger of an Indian attack, not to mention the problem of clearing the ground with their dwindling number of able-bodied men.

Those who feared the Indians most began to favor Clark's Island, but a close examination of it found no fresh water except three of four small pits which were likely to be brackish in summer. Also there was no land cleared for planting corn, and much of the available soil was rocky. Yet the safety of the place attracted many people, and the debate raged far into the night aboard the *Mayflower*.

The next morning, the 20th, they decided to make one more trip ashore. "We could not now take time for further search or consideration," William Bradford says, "our victuals being much spent, especially our beer." They went ashore, surveyed the upriver site, and then took a vote among those who had signed the compact. The majority chose to settle on the mainland, on the shore of the bay where corn land had been cleared, though not planted for three or four years, and "a very sweet brook" ran into the harbor.

There were several places to land shallops and small boats, including the large harborside rock. Best of all, in one field there was a great hill where Miles Standish recommended setting up a platform and planting cannon. From there the defenders could command both the bay and the surrounding countryside, and they could see far out into the bay and even into the sea. There was only one small defect—the cleared land made a long haul in lugging wood. But they decided to make the best of this problem.

Twenty men chose to stay ashore that night. The next day, December 21, every able-bodied man was to join them and begin building houses. But the weather refused to cooperate. That night a storm came howling out of the northeast, and the men on shore could do nothing but shiver and shake through a wet, freezing night. The morning was no better. The bay was so rough that no one could even get off the *Mayflower* to join them. To add to their misery, the men ashore had no food. Finally, some sailors managed to get ashore in the shallop with provisions.

They carried with them a melancholy sight—Richard Britredge of London, sewed into his shroud. He had died at dawn. Braving the wind and rain, they dug a shallow grave for him on the low hill just above the shore. All that day and the next day, Friday, December 22, the storm continued to beat down on the shivering men ashore. That morning aboard the *Mayflower*, there was more gloom. Mary Allerton gave birth to a son, but he was "dead born."

The next day the weather improved and every man well enough to work went ashore and began the laborious task of chopping down pine trees and sawing them into planks for the construction of their first dwelling, a "common house" or "rendezvous." It was to be about twenty feet square and would serve as a shelter for the workers who were to be left ashore each night to guard the precious tools.

The next day, Sunday, no work was done as usual, but those on shore spent some uneasy hours. Early in the morning the woods suddenly erupted with that same unearthly clamor that had signaled an Indian attack on the exploring party two weeks before. Matchlocks were lighted. The men crouched behind their log barricade and waited for the enemy to storm from the forest, but the cries faded away, leaving them only with the eerie sensation of danger. Aboard the *Mayflower* that same day occured another ominous event—the death of Solomon Prower, servant of Christopher Martin.

Monday, December 25, was another working day. These earnest Christians could find no mention of the celebration of Christmas in the Bible, so they simply ignored it. All day they worked, and as twilight was falling, a terrible cry was heard again in the woods. Once more tools were dropped and everyone rushed to his musket, but no attackers leaped from the trees. They left twenty men behind the barricade to keep the night's "court of guard."

Aboard the *Mayflower* there was doleful news. The passengers had drunk the last of their beer. There was nothing left now except the brackish ship's water, but because it was Christmas Day, Christopher Jones donated some of the ship's beer, and sailors and passengers enjoyed a small party together.

That night the weather broke again with "a sore storm of wind and rain," which continued all day Tuesday, the twenty-sixth. But on Wednesday and Thursday everyone was back on shore again, toiling both on the Common House and on the platform on the hill where they planned to set their cannon. On Thursday afternoon, they laid out the measurements for New England's first main street. It was to run up the hill to the fort on top, with two rows of houses on either side. The layout was chosen, probably on Miles Standish's recommendation, because it would be easier to build a palisade around it. To save time and to keep the colony as compact as possible, they decided to assign unmarried men to each family. This reduced the number of houses needed to nineteen. There was a rough attempt to approximate the size of the plots to the size of the families. As for positions on the street, they were chosen by lot.

But the houses were slow in coming. After the first burst of energy, the work bogged down badly. Rain and cold discouraged those on shore. "Great smokes of fire" made by camping Indians further disturbed them. The mile-and-a-half trip from the *Mayflower* to shore was another frustration. The movement of supplies and men was constantly hampered by wind and tide. A ship of the *Speedwell's* size could have come right up to shore, and more than once during these painful days the colonists lamented her loss.

On Monday, January 1, the workers on shore watched the shallop land and sailors lift out the body of another victim, Degory Priest. He was buried beside Richard Britredge on the hill by the shore. It was another grim reminder of the desperate need to get the people off the *Mayflower*. By now the Common House was almost finished, and they went to work on the first of the houses along their main street. Contrary to general belief, they did not build log cabins, which were known only in the Nordic countries in the 1620s and did not appear in the New World until the Swedes settled in Delaware in 1638. The Plymouth colonists built frame houses, about fourteen by eighteen feet with a fireplace along one end and a loft, reached by ladder, for sleeping.

These small houses were not easy to build. A foundation

of stone had first to be laid, then an open frame erected. For this trees had to be cut and trimmed to roughly square sections with a broadax and then finished with an adze. The fireplace and hearth were of fieldstone. For the walls, two-inch planks had to be stripped of their bark and sawed. There was no glass; oil paper was used in the windows, and the joints and cracks in the walls were daubed with clay. For roofs they used thatch, as generations of their country forefathers had done in England. Thatch, however, was not easily gathered at Plymouth. It meant miles of tramping through the meadows and along the creek banks to gather it, with the constant possibility of being cut off by a surprise Indian attack.

It was impossible to forget the Indians, even if they were so inclined. On Wednesday, January 3, they saw more great fires in the distance, coming, they thought, from Indian cornfields. The next day Miles Standish marched with five men in the direction of these fires, hoping to meet the men who made them. But they found only some dilapidated wigwams, long abandoned.

On the way home, however, they had one small piece of luck. They shot an "eagle" out of a tree, and that night all hands enjoyed him for dinner. "It was excellent meat," William Bradford says, "hardly to be discerned from mutton." City dwellers for so long, it was hard for them to learn the hunter's art, and harder still for them to abandon their taste for traditional English food.

They had little interest in fish for food. Captain Jones, who grew up in a port town, thought differently, and when one of his sailors found a herring alive upon the shore, the master had it for supper. Jones urged them to do more fishing, but when they broke out their equipment, he was astonished to find that in their naïveté they had brought the wrong-sized hooks. The ones they had were too large for the kind of fish they could catch in Plymouth Bay, but the considerate captain of the *Mayflower* volunteered to send the shallop out to sea where the fishing might be better.

The shallop fishermen made several trips, and on January 8 they were caught in a violent storm which came close to sinking them. But that night they returned with "three great seals and an excellent good cod." Fresh food could not have been more welcome. The list of sick was growing daily. On January 6 Christopher Martin had become so ill that "to our judgement there was no hope of life." John Carver was called back from shore to confer with the treasurer of the company about his scrambled accounts, but poor Martin was in no condition to discuss finances. Not long before the shallop returned on the eighth, he died, and the next morning he was laid to rest beside the others on the little hill.

Those who had strength continued to build. The big Common House now needed only a roof, but this proved to be slow work. In four days of mixing mortar and gathering thatch, only half of it was finished. The weather continued to be bad, and the discouraged workers found that they were able to use only half their daylight hours.

While toiling on the Common House, sickness struck down one of their strongest and best, William Bradford. He simply collapsed, doubled up with terrific pain, and for a few moments his friends thought he was going to die on the spot. He had been suffering from a severe cold and had felt some pain in his ankles. But now the pain wracked his entire body. Until nightfall his death seemed imminent; then he rallied. But it took him weeks to regain his strength.

Meanwhile some of the younger members of the colony were having adventures. Francis Billington, the lad who had almost blown up the *Mayflower*, remained as itchy as ever. Not long after he came ashore, he shinnied to the top of a tree on a high hill and in the distance saw the sun shining on what appeared to be a great body of water. He was certain he had discovered a sea, perhaps even a Northwest Passage, and pestered the adults until one of the ship's mates took a musket and went with him to find it. After a two-mile walk, they found two lakes, the bigger of them five or six miles around, the smaller, three miles. They seemed to be fresh water and were full of fish. Wild fowl abounded on their banks. Someone in a playful mood named the place Billington Sea, after its impish discoverer.

A few days later, two slightly older members of the colony gave everyone a serious fright. John Goodman and Peter Brown went out with two other men to cut thatch on Friday, January 12. They worked all morning and then sat down to have lunch. They had with them their two dogs, "the great mastiff bitch" and a smaller spaniel. They were only about a mile and a half from the plantation, but the woods were thick and it might as well have been a hundred miles. While the others were still eating, Goodman and Brown decided to do some exploring. Leaving the other two behind to bind the thatch that they had cut, they went off with the dogs.

After lunch, the two who were left behind did as they were told—bound up the thatch and then followed the two explorers. But there was no sign of them. They called and shouted their names. Only echoes drifted back from the silent forest. That was more than enough to raise the hackles on the necks of the two searchers. Indians had seized and perhaps killed Goodman and Brown. They raced back to the plantation with the grim news. John Carver and four other men immediately dropped their work, seized muskets, and rushed into the woods. But there was not a trace of the missing men. The next day Miles Standish and twelve armed men made another search—again fruitless. "They could neither hear nor see anything," Bradford says, "so they returned with much discomfort to us all."

That day Plymouth was full of worried, conferring men. What could they do? If Brown and Goodman were alive and in Indian hands, they had to do something to save them. But how? What? Then late in the afternoon, they heard voices shouting farther down the bay. It was the two lost men with their dogs and they had an adventure story to tell.

Not long after they stepped into the woods, their mastiff had seen a deer. The two dogs bounded off after him, and without thinking the young men ran too. The deer quickly outdistanced all pursuers, but when they had collected the dogs and tried to turn back, they were hopelessly lost. They had wandered all that afternoon, shivering in the rain, without cloaks or hats, no weapons but sickles, and, worst of all, no food. Night soon fell, and with it came snow. They did not know what to do.

But their worries were only beginning. Not long after dark, they had heard what they thought were two lions "roaring exceedingly for a long time together." A third "lion" seemed even closer. They decided to climb a tree, even though it would prove "intolerable cold lodging." All night they walked around and around their selected tree while the "lions" howled and roared in the forest around them. The mastiff bitch was raring to plunge after them, and they had to hold her by the neck. No doubt her growls and snarls and barks were the reason why the wolves never moved in for the attack.

At dawn, the two exhausted men had set out through the forest once more, passing by many lakes and brooks in the woods and in one place a great cleared field which the Indians had burned out, five miles in length. Finally from a high hill they saw Clark's Island in the bay and knew where they were. By the time they reached the colony, they were almost too weak to walk. John Goodman's feet were so frostbitten that his shoes had to be cut off, and he had to be put to bed immediately.

The next day was Sunday, January 14, and it was celebrated with the usual prayer and meditation, both aboard the *Mayflower* and on shore. By now the roof was completed in their Common House, and the workers ashore were using it for a general warehouse and shelter. It was a comforting sight from the ship—the solid-looking walls and fine thatched roof gave the barren shore a hint, at least, of civilization.

But at six o'clock that night an anguished cry of alarm ran through the ship. The Common House was on fire! Everyone immediately thought it was an Indian attack. There was a rush for muskets. Men stormed up ladders and over the side into the shallop, but the tide was too low to land and they had to sit in the big boat for an agonizing three-quarters of an hour, watching the smoke billowing up on shore, wondering if there would be anyone alive when they got there.

They finally arrived to find everyone busy fighting the fire, which was caused not by Indians but by a spark that flew up from the fireplace into the thatch. Fortunately they got it out before any of the beams caught fire, so the roof was still in sound condition.

But it was a close call for William Bradford, who had been lying sick in the house when the fire started. Half-open barrels of gunpowder and charged muskets were lying about the place, and only quick work by Bradford, Goodman, and a few others had gotten them outside before the sparks came raining down. It was a bad scare, and it made them decide to build a separate shed where they could store their provisions and gunpowder beyond the reach of wandering sparks.

A few days later, John Goodman had another adventure in the forest. Limping along on his frostbitten feet, he wandered a little way from the plantation accompanied only by his small spaniel. The dog went frisking ahead of him through the woods, then came scurrying back with frightened, excited yelps. Through the trees loomed two great wolves, obviously intent on making a lunch out of the spaniel.

The little dog cowered between Goodman's legs. The young invalid had no weapon with him, but he picked up a stick and threw it at the two marauders, hitting one. They both ran away, but soon returned, this time creeping stealthily through the trees. Afraid to turn his back, Goodman seized a heavier stick and stood his ground. Both parties maintained their positions " for a good while," the wolves sitting on their tails "grinning at him." Finally, they gave both master and dog up as a bad job and trotted away.

In another week, it was the end of January. The weather continued to alternate between days of rain and sleet and clear winter sunshine. Fortunately, there was no heavy snow. By now they had several houses half completed along the main street, as well as the shed and the Common House. But all through the last week, the work faltered badly, and by the end of the month it had come to a complete stop. In the Common House, aboard the *Mayflower,* and in another small house set aside as an emergency hospital, men and women lay on beds coughing and gasping for breath. The General Sickness had come.

Chapter 11

LOVE AGAINST DEATH

Dozens of persons had been suffering from colds and from the early stages of scurvy, but the continuing state of crisis in which they were living forced many of them to keep going when they should have been in bed. Moreover, scurvy is an extremely deceptive disease with periods when the victim feels quite well and ready to go back to work. Sailors had seen more than one man step from his hammock announcing he was fine, walk a few feet, and drop dead. Now, in the worst of winter, a virus disease similar in many of its symptoms to influenza swept through the weakened colony in epidemic proportions. Bradford, Governor Carver, Winslow, William White, William Mullins, Stephen Hopkins, all were laid low. The victims were so weak that they were unable to perform the simplest physical tasks. At times there were only six or seven out of a hundred people on their feet, and men and women died at the rate of two and three a day.

Dr. Samuel Fuller did what he could to ease their suffering, but the primitive medicine of 1620 had little or no curative powers. His treatment consisted largely of bloodletting, violent physics, and herbal remedies such as the juice of thyme, supposedly specific for bronchial irritations, or lovage, whose leaves, root, and seed were said to cure any sort of fever.

The weather grew worse. During the first week of February there was a violent storm with "the greatest gusts of wind that ever we had." The driving rain melted away most of the clay with which the colonists had daubed their houses, exposing them even more to the weather. So fierce was the storm that even the *Mayflower*, riding cargoless in the harbor, was thought to be in danger.

It was a time of supreme crisis. Lesser men might have given up, left the sick to their doom in the wilderness and sailed for home. But the special spirit that animated these people thrived on challenge. Those who were well worked unceasingly for the sick. "With abundance of toil and hazard of their own health," William Bradford says, "they fetched them wood, made them fires, dressed them meat, made their beds, washed their loathsome clothes, clothed and unclothed them. In a word, did all the homely and necessary offices for them which dainty and queasy stomachs cannot endure to hear named; and all this willingly and cheerfully, without any grudging in the least, showing herein their true love unto their friends and brethren; a rare example and worthy to be remembered." William Brewster and Miles Standish were among the most indefatigable nurses. It is easy enough to see Brewster in the role of the good Samaritan, but that Standish, the tough veteran of the wars, should also play the part was remarkable proof of how deep the spirit of brotherhood ran.

On the *Mayflower* the sick were at first sent ashore—which caused some bitterness among the colonists because ashore they had only water to drink and they thought that beer was helpful medicine. When one of the sailors came ashore, William Bradford asked him for a small flask of beer. The fellow answered curtly, "If you were my own father, you would get none." But when Christopher Jones heard this, he was outraged and sent word ashore to Governor Carver that he should send for beer for anyone that needed it, "though he drunk water homeward bound."

The *Mayflower's* crew soon found they were not immune to the epidemic. It swept through the ship, prostrating almost everyone in the next month. The colonists who were still aboard did what they could to help the sick sailors, and their charity made a profound impression on them. Those like the young boatswain's mate who had scoffed and cursed at the piety of their passengers now found that their "boon companions in drinking and jollity" would not come near them while they lay dying. The boatswain said he did not deserve help from the passengers. He had abused them in word and deed. "You, I now see," he said, "show your love like Christians indeed one to another but we let one another lie and die like dogs."

One sailor spent his last hours cursing his wife, saying if it had not been for her, he never would have made this unlucky voyage. Then he cursed his mates, remembering the money he had loaned them, the help he had given them—and they were now "weary of him." Another man promised his best friend all his possessions when he died, in return for some help. "He went and got a little spice and made him a mess of meat once or twice," Bradford says, "and because he died not so soon as he expected, he went among his fellows and swore . . . he would see him choked before he made him any more meat; and yet the poor fellow died before morning."

During this terrible time, while he slowly recovered from his own sickness, William Bradford began his career as a historian. He started to jot in his notebook small things that happened, beginning at first with little more than a melancholy record of deaths. "Jan. 21. Dies Rose, the wife of Capt. Standish . . . N.B. This month 8 of our number die." What was it that stirred this young, comparatively uneducated man to record the details—and eventually the lives—of these humble people? Was it a reaction to his wife's death? Did he wish to expiate his personal failure by assuming a larger responsibility? Or did he sense in the depths of their unlovely anguish the magnificence of their spirit? Perhaps both, perhaps neither. But these primitive notes were another step in William Bradford's commitment to a lifetime of service.

February was Plymouth's worst month. Seventeen persons died. Work came to a complete standstill. The weather continued to be miserably cold and rainy. On February 9, during an especially bad cold spell, another spark from a fire kindled the roof of one of the small houses that was being used as a hospital. As before, the sick had to flee into the cold, but the fire was "quickly doused with no great harm done." That same day Captain Jones, still anxious to do what he could to ease his friends' suffering, went ashore and killed five geese which he distributed among the sick.

On that same hunting trip Jones found something more ominous in the woods—"a good deer" killed by the Indians and left to be eaten by the wolves; the savages had contented themselves with cutting off the horns. It was another unnerving reminder that the Indians were all around them. Ten days before, Captain Jones and his sailors had spotted two braves studying the *Mayflower* from Saquish Head. They tried to communicate with the silent visitors, but the savages quickly slipped away. On February 16, there was a far more serious alarm. One of the few healthy men went into the woods to hunt for fresh food. Crouching in the reeds by Jones River about a mile and a half from the plantation, he was horrified to see twelve Indians pad silently past him in single file heading toward Plymouth. In the woods nearby he heard the noise of many more.

Wisely the hunter lay absolutely quiet until they passed, then raced home to give the alarm. For a moment it looked like the final disaster. The few men still on their feet, such as Miles Standish and Francis Cooke, were working in the forest cutting firewood for the sick. Shouts from the plantation brought them back at top speed, and for several hours the handful of defenders crouched at the probable points of attack around the colony, waiting for the savage onslaught.

But once more the woods remained silent. Not a single red man appeared. Not even a war whoop was heard. Only toward evening did they see signs of a great fire burning along the creek near where the hunter had discovered the Indians. Standish and Cooke now went back into the woods to get their axes and saws and found, to their great chagrin, that the stealthy visitors had stolen them.

The next day, they held a council of war "for the establishing of military orders." They chose Miles Standish as their captain and gave him absolute authority in military affairs. Standish immediately ordered a refurbishing of muskets and armour which, with the sickness and heavy construction, had been left to the mercy of wind and rain and were in deplorable condition. As they listened to the captain lecture them on weapons and other military matters, their conference was interrupted by the appearance of two gaudily painted braves upon the top of a hill less than a quarter of a mile away on the other side of the Town Brook.

They stood there emblazoned against the sky, while the little band of white men stared at them in silent astonishment. Then the Indians began making gestures. The white men, totally unused to their sign language, took several minutes to decide that they were inviting them up on the hill for a parley. The colonists made similar signs inviting the Indians to visit them, but the results was negative. The red men did not move a foot.

All this was at the height of the General Sickness and there could not have been more than a dozen men on their feet. Nevertheless Standish and Stephen Hopkins decided that they would cross the Town Brook and accept the Indians' invitation. Only Standish carried his musket, but the rest of the men held their guns ready while the two ambassadors crossed the shallow brook and began to mount the hill.

Captain Standish made an elaborate performance of placing his musket on the ground in full sight of the savages "in sign of peace." But the two white men were wearing their armour and had swords at their belts. The sight of them clanking up the hill was too much for the Indians, and just before Standish and Hopkins reached speaking distance, they turned and ran. In the forest behind the hill there were sounds of a small stampede indicating that there were many more braves backing up these ambassadors.

This strange performance, which seemed to be mixed equally with hostility and fear, enabled Miles Standish to turn the colony's labors toward military defense for a few days. On the hill behind their houses, they finally finished the construction of a sturdy platform with emplacements for cannon. They had already brought one cannon ashore from the *Mayflower*, a saker, but they lacked the manpower to haul its fifteen hundred pounds up the hill and wrestle it into place on the platform.

On Wednesday, February 21, Christopher Jones came ashore with many of his sailors and brought with him one of his "great pieces" called a minion. Sailors and colonists together dragged this twelve-hundred-pound monster and their saker up the hill and secured them in position. They also emplaced two smaller cannon called bases. When the work was finished, Captain Standish strode back and forth across the platform with a highly satisfied air. From this vantage point, these guns could sweep the surrounding forests and the harbor. Plymouth had taken a long stride toward survival.

But the sickness continued to ravage them. February 21 was one of their worst days. In his Pocket Book, William Bradford somberly noted: "Feb. 21. Die Mr. William White, Mr. William Mullins, with 2 more." Mullins made a will, leaving his twenty-five-dozen pairs of shoes and thirteen pairs of boots to the joint stock company for forty pounds, if "they like them at that rate." He divided his estate equally between his wife, two sons (one still in England), and daughter Priscilla, and appointed John Carver and "Mr. Williamson" as his executors, asking them also "to have an eye over my wife and children to be as fathers and friends to them." That this "stranger" from London should ask this of John Carver and William Brewster shows how close the two groups had grown in their common toil and suffering.

Like the others who had died, these two leaders were buried at night on the hill above the rock in shallow, unmarked graves. Convinced that the Indians were watching them constantly, the colonists were afraid that if their mysterious hosts saw how fearfully death was decimating them, it would be an invitation to attack. If only they could somehow communicate with these red men and let them know they wanted peace! But how can you talk to a will-o'-the-wisp, a face on the hill, a fleeting shape in the forest, a haunting cry by night? For the time being they could only bury their dead and endure.

Chapter 12

WELCOME!

The month of March began hopefully. On the third, the wind shifted to the south, and after a misty morning the sun came out, and it was a warm, fair, almost springlike day. "The birds sang in the woods most pleasantly," William Bradford tells us. But sickness continued to plague them, and work on the remaining houses moved forward slowly. Four months after their arrival in the New World, some of their people were still living on the *Mayflower*. Wednesday, March 7, was another good day, colder than the third but fair and sunny. It looked so promising that several families decided to plant garden seeds around their houses.

A few days later the colonists had to deal with their first case of public discipline. Every able-bodied man was required to stand watch during the night on a rotating basis under the direction of Miles Standish. But when John Billington's turn came he damned the captain and swore he was not going to lose his sleep looking for invisible Indians.

Standish instantly put Billington under arrest, and he was called before the whole company, with Governor John Carver sitting as judge.

Carver ordered him punished by having his neck and heels tied together—a relatively mild sentence compared to what Standish was undoubtedly recommending. Before the trial was over, Billington's bravado melted away, and he humbly promised to obey the captain's orders henceforth. Since it was his first offense, Governor Carver quickly commuted his sentence. It might have been better for Billington if he had been treated with Standish's severity. This was the first of many offenses for this quarrelsome man. He was continually clashing with those in authority. At one point he was involved in a plot to overthrow the government by armed revolt. Finally, in 1630, he had a bitter quarrel with a recent arrival, one John Newcomen, waylaid him in a lonely part of the forest and shot him dead. Billington was tried by a jury of his peers for Newcomen's murder, and became the first American to die at the end of a hangman's rope.

Billington's first rebellion prompted the colonists to complete their conference on Military Orders which they had begun in the previous month and had been interrupted by the appearance and disappearance of the sign-language ambassadors beyond the brook. Once more the men gathered in the Common House to draw up the rules and regulations which Captain Standish said he needed for the security of the colony.

But they had only begun to talk when out of the woods strode a tall, handsome Indian wearing nothing but a fringe of leather about his waist. While the white men stared in amazement, the red man came straight toward them up their main street as casually and calmly as a Sunday stroller out for a promenade. They met him at the door of the Common House; otherwise he would have certainly walked right in. There was an awkward pause; then the Indian stepped back, raised his hand in friendly salute, and said "Welcome!"

The colonists were struck dumb. After all these months of pursuing at a distance, exchanging signs, following cold trails, here was an Indian standing in their doorway speaking English!

Manfully suppressing their joy, they greeted the visitor with gravity, but made it clear he was welcome. He promptly amazed them by asking for some beer. They explained that there was none, but they offered him brandy, biscuit, butter and cheese, some pudding, and a piece of a mallard. To their astonishment, he ate them all. Where had he acquired his taste for English food? Eagerly they began to question him "of many things." His English was somewhat broken, but he knew enough to explain that he had learned their language and tasted their food among the English fishermen who had visited his country off and on over the last four or five years. To prove it, he was able to name a dozen or so captains and mates whom he had met.

His country was Morattigon (present-day Pemaquid Point, Maine), and he was one of the Sagamores or lords of the Algonkian there. His name was Samoset, and he had been visiting for the past eight months in these parts. He had sailed down the coast with a Captain Dermer, a name the colonists knew well. He had been sent out by the Council for New England to explore the coast, but he had not returned when the colonists sailed from Plymouth. Samoset seemed to have had no special reason for coming with Dermer beyond a simple love of travel. He had apparently made many similar trips since he knew the whole country between Plymouth and Maine. "He discoursed," Bradford tells us, "of every Province and of their Sagamores and their number of men and strength."

All this time he had been standing in the doorway of the Common House. The white men were a little leery about letting this tall, husky Indian inside the building. The March wind whipped at them, and they offered Samoset a "horseman's coat," assuming that in his naked state he was freezing to death.

Now they questioned him about Plymouth. Where were the Indians who lived here and had cleared these cornfields but failed to plant them in recent years? Gravely Samoset explained that in the Indian language this place was called Patuxet, and here there had lived a tribe that were numerous and strong. They had been hostile to white men and barbarously murdered everyone that landed on their shores. But four years ago an extraordinary plague had broken out among them. Every man, woman, and child had died. The entire tribe had been wiped out, and nearby tribes, certain that the place was haunted by evil spirits, had shunned the land, so there was no one to contest their possession or lay claim to it.

Samoset also gave the colonists a clear picture of their neighbors. The nearest were the Wampanoags, a small tribe of about sixty warriors headed by a wise chief named Massasoit, who largely through skillful diplomacy was also the ruling sachem of numerous minor tribes in the area. He had been Samoset's host for the past eight months. To the northeast, out on Cape Cod, were the Nausets with about a hundred warriors. They were the ones who had attacked the colonists on their third voyage of discovery.

Last July, Samoset told them, the Nausets had attacked Captain Dermer and his men and had slain three of them. They hated the English because several years before, one Captain Hunt, a fisherman who visited their shores, lured seven of their men and twenty of the Patuxets aboard his ship on pretense of wanting to trade and then kidnapped them to Spain where he sold them as slaves for twenty pounds a man.

The colonists spent the whole afternoon talking to Samoset. When night began to fall he presented a problem. They would have "gladly been rid of him," but he showed no indications of going. They finally decided he ought to go aboard the *Mayflower.* They were not at all sure about trusting his friendly manner. He might be a spy under orders to attack them from behind while his friends charged from the forest. But Samoset was perfectly content to go aboard the ship, and he climbed into the shallop without a murmur.

However, the wind was high and the tide was out and the shallop proved impossible to launch. They had to take their visitor back into the settlement and lodge him at Stephen Hopkins' house. A man stood guard outside the house all night with orders to kill Samoset if he made a single hostile move. But the chief slept the sleep of the innocent and the next morning rose early announcing that he would return to Massasoit, his host.

The colonists gave him a knife, a bracelet, and a ring as

testimony of friendship and urged him to bring with him some of Massasoit's tribe, hopefully with beaver skins to trade. If they came, they were to leave their bows and arrows a quarter of a mile away, as a sign of peace.

The next day Samoset returned, bringing with him five tall braves. They were better dressed than their guide, each wearing deer skin and long leather leggings which ran from ankles to waist. One wore a feather in his hair, another a fox's tail. All were highly painted, some with long black stripes on their faces, others with more ingenious decorations.

The colonists greeted the visitors outside the town and found that they had abandoned their bows and arrows as directed. In the little settlement, everyone gathered around, and both sides exchanged sign language of "friendship and amity." They offered the Indians food, and "they did eat liberally of our English victuals." In return they sang and danced for the white men. They had brought with them four or five beaver skins, but because it was Sunday, the colonists could not trade with them.

Diplomatically they explained to the Indians, using Samoset as their interpreter, that they wished them to bring more skins and then they would trade freely and generously for all. The Indians promised to return within a night or two and, as proof of their trust, said they would leave behind the skins they had brought, which they did, over the protests of the colonists. The red men also promised to return the tools that Standish and his assistant had left in the woods.

Well satisfied with their diplomatic progress, the colonists gave the Indians a guard of honor back to where they had left their bows and arrows. Unfortunately, this disturbed the red men more than it pleased them. They suspected they were going to be murdered when they reached a certain distance from the plantation, and two began to "slink away." But the others called them back, and they reached their weapons without further incident. Both sides parted with smiles and kind words, and the Indians again promised they would return soon.

Samoset declined to go back with his friends. He said he was sick, but something in his manner made the colonists suspect he was faking. Whatever the real reason, the Algonkian chief remained with them until Wednesday morning, while the white men waited anxiously for the return of his friends. They finally persuaded Samoset to go to the Wampanoags and renew communications. They gave him a hat, a pair of stockings and shoes, a shirt, and a loin cloth, which was the only thing he deigned to wear.

More than contented, Samoset departed, and the colonists settled down once more to work out their Military Orders, which had been twice interrupted by the unexpected arrival of Indians. This conference seemed to have a magic ability to produce red men. After little more than an hour of conferring, three warriors appeared on the top of the hill across the brook. They were wearing their most brilliant war paint, and they leaped about the hilltop sharpening and rubbing their arrows together in what seemed to the white man a show of defiance. Captain Standish and William Bradford took their muskets, donned armor, and crossed the Town Brook to confer with them. Two mates from the *Mayflower* followed, without armor but carrying muskets. Once again as the white men drew near, the Indians scampered into the woods.

Considerably irritated, the colonists went back to their military conference and this time finished it. Later in the day they finished another task on which they had long been toiling. Their carpenter, who had been down with the General Sickness, made some much needed repairs to the shallop, and they sailed it out to the *Mayflower* and brought back the last of those who had been living aboard for almost six long months. The day was March 21.

That same day, William Bradford made another mournful entry in his Pocket Book: "March 21. Dies Elizabeth, the wife of Mr. Edward Winslow. N.B. This month, thirteen of our number die." The sickness continued to rage, though its virulence was diminishing. The survivors were slow to regain their strength, but they could at last begin to think in terms of survival and estimate the ghastly effects of the plague on their prospects.

The long death toll included thirteen of eighteen wives. Several families were totally wiped out, including Christopher Martin, his wife, and stepson Solomon Prower, and Edward and John Tilley, courageous volunteers for the third exploration and their wives. Priscilla Mullins lost father, mother, and brother. Among the single men, hired hands, and servants, the mortality was terrible. Nineteen of twenty-nine died, including the young wanderer and bridegroom John Goodman. The children proved sturdier than the adults. Of seven girls, none died, and of thirteen boys, only three. One of the few families that escaped unscathed was the Billingtons—the most irreligious members of the little colony. After such remarkably good health on the long voyage, death had now reduced their numbers by half. The unmarked graves on the seaside hill had swelled to almost fifty.

March 22 was fair and warm, carrying on its breezes more promises of early spring. Even more hopeful was the return of Samoset from his diplomatic mission, bringing with him another Indian who had an even more fascinating personal story to tell. His name was Tisquantum, but he was called Squanto. He was the only living member of the Patuxet tribe, having survived, ironically, through the treachery of Captain Hunt, who had carried him and the other braves away to Spain to be sold into slavery.

Years before, in 1605, Squanto had already made a trip to England with another early visitor to Plymouth harbor, Captain George Weymouth. He had returned to the New World with Captain John Smith when that doughty explorer had mapped the coast of New England. Squanto was thus prepared to shift for himself, and when he was sold as a slave in Malaga, he quickly talked his way into the hands of the local friars, who decided he was an excellent prospect for conversion.

Somehow, in the course of a year or two, Squanto managed to attach himself to an Englishman traveling in Spain, and he arrived in England, where he was well received by many people, including the powerful Sir Ferdinando Gorges, head of the Council for New England. Thanks to Gorges, Squanto had been sent back to his native land with Captain Dermer in 1619, but had arrived to discover that his family and entire tribe had been wiped out by the plague that Samoset had already described.

Squanto spoke more English than Samoset, and he informed the white men that the great Sagamore Massasoit was nearby in the woods along with his brother Quadequina and all their braves—some sixty in number. But the ambassador had trouble explaining just what the great chief wanted. Finally, he retired for further consultation, and in about an hour an awesome sight appeared on the hill beyond the brook.

The chief himself strode out of the woods, wearing about his neck his badge of office, a great chain of white bone beads. His face was dyed a deep mulberry, and he was oiled from head to foot so that his body gleamed in the sun. Behind him came sixty tall, grim-looking warriors, all painted on the face and body, some black, some red, some yellow, some white and some with crosses and others with grotesque loops and squares. A few wore skins. Many were naked. All were tall muscular-looking men. Did they know that they outnumbered the white men three or four to one? The colonists could only grip their muskets and hope for the best.

The ambassador, Squanto, reported that the great chief wished them to send someone to "parley" with him. The colonists had a hurried conference and decided it would be unwise to send Governor Carver. But Edward Winslow, only twenty-five, volunteered to make the risky trip across the brook. It would be the first of his many diplomatic achievements on behalf of Plymouth.

Buckling on his armor and sword, Winslow crossed the brook and marched bravely up the hill. Solemnly he presented to Massasoit a pair of knives and a copper chain with a jewel in it. To Quadequina he gave a knife and a jewel to hang in his ear. Next came a pot of brandy and some biscuits and butter. The chief accepted the gifts in silence but with great dignity. Winslow then made a brief speech in which he told Massasoit that King James saluted him with words of love and peace and wished him for a friend and ally. He also said that Governor Carver wished to parley with him in Plymouth and to arrange a treaty of trade and peace.

Squanto and Samoset interpreted the speech as best they could and the chief seemed to approve, although Winslow was somewhat dismayed by their brief translation. The chief then sampled the food and drink and passed most of it on to his warriors. He next expressed great admiration for Winslow's sword and armor as well as a desire to buy it, but Winslow was able politely to decline without giving offense.

Finally Massasoit decided to leave Winslow in the custody of Quadequina and forty of his braves. He ordered the other twenty warriors to leave their bows and arrows behind them and accompany him into Plymouth. Captain Standish and William Brewster met the chief at the Town Brook with a half dozen musketeers as a guard of honor. They exchanged salutes and marched together down the little main street to an unfinished house. There they had spread a green rug and three or four cushions. The chief and his most important warriors sat down on these, and then Governor Carver appeared, preceded by a drum and a trumpet and another guard of honor. Miles Standish was the stage manager for this performance. He was determined to impress the Indians with all the military pomp and bravado that his handful of soldiers could muster.

Governor Carver kissed Massasoit's hand on entering, and the chief returned the compliment. They then sat down, and Carver offered the chief a drink of brandy. He took a great swallow, enough to scald his insides, but his grave expression remained unchanged. The white men noticed, however, that it made him sweat considerably. Next they served some fresh meat, which the chief sampled and passed on to his followers. The chief now drew some tobacco from a bag that he wore around his neck. He lit a pipe and took some puffs and passed it to the white men. Then, through their interpreters, Squanto and Samoset, they began to discuss a treaty of peace.

With no difficulty, they worked out a mutual-assistance pact that remains a model of its kind. There were seven clauses.

1. That neither he nor any of his should injure or do hurt to any of our people.

2. And if any of his did hurt to any of ours; he should send the offender to us that we might punish him.

3. That if any of our tools were taken away when our people were at work; he should cause them to be restored: and if ours did any harm to any of his we would do the like to them.

4. If any did unjustly war against him; we would aid him. If any did war against us, he should aid us.

5. He should send to his neighboring confederates to certify them of this, that they might not wrong us; but might be likewise compromised in the conditions of peace.

6. That when their men came to us, they should leave their bows and arrows behind them; as we should do our pieces when we came to them.

7. Lastly, that doing this King James would esteem of him as his friend and ally.

Massasoit accepted all these clauses and repeated them to his followers who were equally pleased by them. The parley over, Governor Carver conducted Massasoit to the brook. There they embraced each other, but the colonists detained six or seven braves as hostages until Edward Winslow was returned by the Indians. After a short wait, however, Squanto returned, informing them that not Winslow but Quadequina was coming. Apparently the brother of the great chief wished to be entertained in equally royal fashion.

Miles Standish marched another guard of honor to meet Quadequina, and he was greeted by Governor Carver in the half-finished house. He was, however, extremely leery of the white men's muskets and made sounds of dislike, asking that they be taken away. Standish, showing himself diplomat as well as soldier, quickly complied. So they entertained Quadequina with brandy and fresh meat and such conversation as was possible in spite of the language barrier. "He was a very proper, tall young man," William Bradford says, "of a very modest and seemly countenance." He seemed to appreciate the entertainment and left them at the Town Brook with great expressions of friendship.

Two of his friends were so delighted by the reception that they were inclined to stay behind for the night, but the colonists made it clear that they would not permit this. They allowed Samoset and Squanto to stay, however, and from them they learned that Massasoit and all his men, as well as their women and children, were spending the night in the woods not half a mile from Plymouth.

Standish promptly posted extra guards. The captain was

still worried about a surprise attack. But the darkness passed into dawn without a sign of trouble, and in the morning many braves came over the Town Brook in a most friendly manner in search of food. They let the white men know that the chief wished someone to visit him for a further parley. Miles Standish and Isaac Allerton made the trip alone and were graciously welcomed and given three or four ground nuts and some tobacco. Of serious parleying there was none. Apparently Massasoit merely wished the white men to come to him as he had come to them.

From the talkative Squanto they also learned that Massasoit needed them as much as they needed him. He was frequently at war with the powerful Narragansetts and hoped that the white men with their guns of thunder would be strong allies. In the next few weeks, as Indians and white men met in the woods, singly and in pairs, without the least sign of hostility, the spirit of mutual trust and confidence between the two peoples grew steadily.

Chapter 13

A SPECIAL INSTRUMENT
FOR THEIR GOOD

During April the weather continued to improve
and so did their relations with the Wampanoags. In fact,
relations became almost too good. Although Massasoit, the
great chief, returned home to his headquarters at Sowams,
some forty miles away, many of his warriors and their families
lingered in the vicinity of Plymouth and began appearing
at the town gates with monotonous regularity in search of
food and trinkets. The colonists were loath to offend them and
entertained them as best they could, but their supply of food
and gifts was meager, and it soon became apparent that somehow this constant visiting would have to be halted.

One red man, however, did not wear out his welcome.
This was Squanto, who in his two trips to England seemed
to have acquired a considerable fondness for the ways of
the white man. He showed no desire to return to Sowams
with Massasoit, and he soon made himself invaluable in
Plymouth. His first performance came on March 23. It was

a sunny day, and at noon Squanto announced that he was going to fish for eels. He went down to a nearby river at low tide and came back at nightfall with all the eels he could carry. The colonists found them delightful eating—"fat and sweet." They begged Squanto to tell how he caught them, and he readily demonstrated how he squashed them out of the mud with his feet and caught them with his hands.

This was only the beginning of Squanto's good offices. It soon became apparent to the colonists that he was, in Bradford's words, "a special instrument of God for their good." Early in April when the colonists began to prepare for spring planting, Squanto gave them the crucial warning that unless they fertilized their corn ground with fish the whole crop would come to nothing. This caused vast consternation. The white men were depending solely on their corn crop to get them through the following winter, but they had as yet caught only one lonely cod. Where were they going to get the fish to do the fertilizing?

Calmly Squanto assured them that in the middle of April the Town Brook would be swarming with alewives coming to spawn. They could be caught by the hundreds, and they made excellent manure. Exactly on schedule the fish came and were caught under Squanto's expert direction. Next he showed them how to set the fish in the ground, three to each hill of five corn kernels with the fish heads close to the seeds. He also warned his new friends that unless they set a guard over the cornfields for the next fourteen nights—until the fish became rotten in the ground—the wolves would creep out of the forest and dig them up. So the guard was set and the wolves were frustrated and the corn crop began to prosper.

According to the old Julian calendar, which the colonists followed, March 25 was the first day of the year. On this day they had re-elected John Carver as governor for a full year. Eleven days later Governor Carver made the first major decision of his new term: he let the *Mayflower* sail for home. As William Bradford explained, the governor "seeing so many die and fall down sick daily thought it no wisdom to send away the ship, their condition considered and their danger from the Indians, till they could procure some shelter and therefore thought it better to draw some more charge on themselves and friends than to hazard all."

For his part Jones had no inclination to chance a winter voyage with half his crew sick. Even now he was leaving ten of his best men in the shallow graves on the hill above the harbor. But he could not afford to stay any longer without risking a starvation voyage home. One thing is certain: Christopher Jones sailed with the best wishes of these men and women whom he had carried to America, wishes that he wholeheartedly reciprocated. The longer he knew them, the better he liked them, and the history of their friendship was a continuous growth of mutual respect. Only a few writers have appreciated the vital part that the personality and courage of the master of the *Mayflower* played in the founding of Plymouth; fewer still have discerned the friendship that gradually grew between colonists and captain in spite of the differences in their backgrounds, the hostility of the crew, and the frustrations of the long voyage.

Sailing at a better season, the *Mayflower* would be home in four weeks. Within the year Christopher Jones would be dead, weakened, many think, by the exposure and hardship he endured while exploring the shores of Cape Cod and Plymouth harbor. Within another year the *Mayflower* herself would be a moldering wreck in a nautical bone yard, sold for little more than the value of her sails and rigging.

But on April 5, 1621, as she stood out of Plymouth harbor, the old freighter meant only one thing to the colonists who watched her. Their last link with home, their last refuge was going. Many men and women wept unashamedly, but not a single person demanded passage home aboard the *Mayflower*. Seldom in the previous history of English colonization had a ship sailed for home without a scramble among the fainthearted for passage aboard her. But these men and women were lifted up by a purpose larger than themselves, larger than their individual gains or losses. Strangers and saintly brethren from Leyden were now bound by common suffering, common courage, into a unique solidarity.

What made the commitment of these people even more remarkable was the awful gaps that had been torn in their ranks by the General Sickness. There were widows like Susanna White and widowers like Edward Winslow who had special motives for giving up in despair. The plague had left intact only four couples—the Billingtons, the Hopkinses, the Brewsters and the Carvers. The man who had perhaps the strongest motive to return was William Bradford. His son was waiting for him in Holland. His wife lay beneath the cold waters off Cape Cod. But the idea does not seem to have occured to him. His heart and soul were consumed now in the larger vision, the struggle of a whole people; he had seen its birth in the worst days of the sickness, when distinctions between leaders and led, Londoners and Leydeners, had vanished, and they had fought with all their strength, not for individual but for common survival. "Whilst they had health—yea or any strength continuing," Bradford wrote later, "they were not wanting to any that had need of them. And I doubt not but their recompense is with the Lord." Who could desert such people?

Among the many letters Christopher Jones undoubtedly carried to friends in the Old World, there was one written by Governor John Carver to Sir Ferdinando Gorges and the Council for New England, asking them for a patent confirming the colonists right to settle in Plymouth and govern themselves as they saw fit. All during these months of agonizing struggle, this threat hung constantly over their heads. If Gorges and his friends failed to receive the royal seal of approval, they would have no power to grant this legalization—and the news could stir all the latent rebellion among the servants and wayward spirits of the colony, such as the Billingtons. Until their choice of Plymouth was confirmed, a shadow of uncertainty would hang over all their plans and decisions. It did not make life any easier.

For the rest of April the colony worked hard at planting their corn under Squanto's direction. During this crucial month the general routine of Plymouth's early years gradually established itself. The days were spent in the innumerable small tasks which absorbs so much of life on any frontier. The fields had to be tended constantly. Most of the men and many of the women were assigned to them each day. Others were sent regularly to hunt and fish. The carpenters and others handy with their tools such as John Alden made furniture and put finishing touches on the houses and public buildings. The women were kept busy with cooking and washing and with repairing the precious supply of clothes, which there was small chance of replenishing for years to come. In their precious spare time, they toiled on the vegetable gardens around the houses.

Each Sunday, at the beat of a drum, the entire town assembled in the main street, and with every man carrying his musket, they followed Governor Carver to the Common House where they attended church services. For the occasion, Carver probably wore his fine red cloak, and everyone else had on good if not their best clothes. Their colors were by no means the drab black and browns they supposedly favored. These people were Elizabethans and loved color in their dress. There were blue, red, and green cloaks and smocks. William Brewster had a violet suit and another man had a "saten" suit and "sky colored garters," as well as "a cap with silver lace on it." The "bands," flat white collars worn by the men, were white and glistening. Some men and women favored the high crowned hats often pictured in traditional paintings, but they were by no means universally worn.

In church, Elder Brewster served as pastor. Since he was not ordained, he was unable to give communion, but he was an excellent preacher. William Bradford says that, "in teaching he was very stirring, and moving the affections; also very plain and distinct in what he taught; by which means he became the more profitable to the hearers. He had a singular good gift in prayer . . . in ripping up the heart and conscience before God. . . . He always thought it were better for ministers to pray oftener, and divide their prayers, than to be long and tedious in the same."

Brewster preferred to dwell on God's love and mercy rather than on His wrath. The Ruling Elder's influence reached deep into Plymouth's life, making the colony famous for the mildness of its laws. Like his disciple Bradford, he was of the opinion that no church had a monopoly on religious truth, and he despised the religious contentions that were ripping Europe apart.

If we judge them by the standards of the 1960s, of course, the leaders of Plymouth could be (and have been) painted as intolerant. They did not encourage men and women of differing beliefs to settle in Plymouth. They were trying to create an ideal community, and within its boundaries they felt unanimity of religious belief was essential to achieving that goal. But they were perfectly willing to accept other men of differing beliefs as equals, outside Plymouth, or when they came to the colony as visitors. In later years they invariably pursued this live-and-let-live policy both with the easygoing Dutch in New York and the stern Puritans around Boston, with whom modern Americans have unfortunately confused them. At a time when harboring a Catholic priest was a death sentence in England, some French Jesuits visited Plymouth and were received with every courtesy. Although Brewster and his congregation ate meat on Friday to underscore their Protestantism, the Ruling Elder even saw to it that the Reverend Fathers were served fish.

The hard labor in the cornfields soon caused a tragic loss. In spite of their ages, Governor Carver and William Brewster insisted on taking hoes and spades and working away at the planting with the rest. While Brewster had the rugged physique of the countryman, Carver had spent most of his adult life as a sedentary merchant. One particularly hot day in mid-April Carver suddenly dropped his hoe and complained of a terrific pain in the head. Everyone assumed that he had had too much sun. But he went into his house and lay down and in a few hours lapsed into a coma. He died within a few days and was buried with a guard of honor and a volley of small arms over his grave. His wife, a frail woman who was totally dependent on him, died about five weeks later. They generously left their entire estate to their servant, John Howland, who promptly bought his freedom and began a long life as one of Plymouth's leaders.

Now came a crucial choice for the fifty surviving members of the colony. They must elect a new governor. Carver had been an easy choice. He had been an older man, a successful merchant, a leading member of the church in Leyden. Now they must choose another man of no "special eminency" from their thinned ranks. The logical person, if personal qualities were the only consideration, might seem to be William Brewster. But he was automatically eliminated by his position as ruling elder of the church.

One of these people's deepest convictions was the necessity for maintaining careful separation between church and state. They had experienced at cruelly close range the disastrous effects of its union in England. So it was necessary to choose a man who had no churchly role. They also sensed that he had to be a man who would be more realistic and energetic than John Carver, who hesitated about so many things and hence often allowed decisions to relapse into undirected debates.

Unanimously, the choice fell on William Bradford. It was in part a testament of gratitude for his leadership in bringing them to this fruitful, fortunate harbor. But it was also proof of his friends' confidence in his dedication to their common enterprise. His election was the beginning of Bradford's thirty-five years of service to Plymouth. From 1621 until his death in 1657, he was re-elected governor or assistant governor more than thirty times, serving without salary for most of his terms.

From Bradford's first days in office a new vigor entered Plymouth's public affairs. The younger men who had volunteered for the great adventure in the New World now assumed their rightful leadership. Edward Winslow, Stephen Hopkins, Miles Standish, John Alden, all in their thirties or younger, would be Bradford's staunch and energetic supporters in the years to come.

Perhaps Bradford's greatest achievement was his revision of the colony's economic organization in 1623. Spurred by hunger, the colonists had worked hard in the fields during their first year, but in succeeding years it became more and more difficult to get them to put their best efforts into this essential task. Bradford decided that the reason was the stipulation in their contract with the London merchants that everything in the colony, including the crops, was to be held in common for seven years. This crude communism was crippling individual enterprise. Boldly, on his own authority, Bradford abandoned the arrangement and announced that henceforth every family would raise its own corn. Plymouth never went hungry again. To Bradford this proved "the vanity of that conceit . . . that the taking away of property and bringing in community into a commonwealth would make [men] happy and flourishing."

Chapter 14

Duels and diplomacy

The month of May began auspiciously with Plymouth's first marriage. Governor Bradford performed the ceremony binding Susanna White, a widow of three months, and Edward Winslow, a widower of two months. The soft, sweet warmth of New England's spring was all about them, and Plymouth was delighted to have something to celebrate after the long winter of sickness, disaster, and gloom.

One of the most misleading myths about these early Americans is their supposed indifference to enjoying life. They took their religion seriously, to be sure. But they also relished good food, good liquor, and good conversation. Like all Elizabethans they loved music, and the Psalms were by no means the only songs they sang. At the Winslow wedding feast they undoubtedly showed their skill at singing those complex songs for many voices called madrigals. Some were simple ditties, no more profound than a modern popular song.

My bonnie lass she smileth
And she my heart beguileth
Smile less, dear love, therefore
And you shall love me more.

Other songs were straight humor.

Willie prithee go to bed
For thou wilt have a drowsy head
Tomorrow we must ahunting and betimes be stirring
With a hey ho traloly.

Others approached fine poetry.

Weep you no more sad fountains
What need you flow so fast
Look how the snowy mountains
Heavens sun doth gently waste
But my sun's heavenly eyes
View not your weeping
That now lies sleeping
Now softly lies sleeping.

Many similar marriages would take place in the next few years as various members of the colony recovered from their personal sorrows. William Bradford would marry again in 1623, choosing as his wife the widow of a friend from the Leyden church. John Alden would marry Priscilla Mullins in 1622 without any of the romantic diplomacy for which Henry Wadsworth Longfellow made them famous. If Captain Miles Standish ever expressed any interest in the young Priscilla, the evidence is lost to history. The captain also remarried again in 1623, choosing, according to one tradition, the younger sister of his dead wife Rose.

Throughout the months of May and June the colonists concentrated on finishing the houses they needed and regaining their health in the spring sunshine. The three families still intact were each allotted houses, and they each took in several single men and women. Young Priscilla Mullins, for instance, lived with Elder Brewster and his family. The other four houses were divided among the remaining single persons. During these same months the colonists completed two other houses which they planned to use as storerooms, giving them a total of four public houses and seven dwellings. This was just enough to keep them going—the General Sickness had left so many weak that they decided against the heavy labor involved in any more building.

Life in these tiny one-and-a-half-room dwellings was difficult. The entire house was not much bigger than the average living room today. There was the low room under the eaves for sleeping, but waking hours, during bad weather, had to be spent in the crowded quarters below. Stephen Hopkins' household was typical. Beneath his small roof he crowded two children by his first wife, thirteen-year-old Giles and fifteen-year-old Constance, three-year-old Damaris and six-month-old Oceanus and their mother Elizabeth, as well as his two servants Edward Dotey and Edward Leister.

According to family tradition Constance was a pretty girl with her father's high spirits. Dotey and Leister, equally high spirited—they had been among the chief mutterers of mutiny before the compact was signed—soon found themselves competing ferociously for a kind word from her. It was an age when falling in love was considered a fatal disease, useless to resist, and these two young bravoes were perfect prospects for all the worst symptoms. Soon, where there had been easy camaraderie and friendship, there was sullen jealousy. Young Constance, childishly playing at courtly love, coyly encouraged the strife, never suspecting she was close to becoming an accomplice to a murder.

At dawn on June 18, Dotey and Leister seized their swords and daggers and crept quietly out of the crowded house. Down the beach to a deserted stretch of sand they stalked. There, sword in one hand, dagger in the other, they began Plymouth's first duel. Snarling, cursing, they raged up and down the shore. Dotey sank his rapier deep into Leister's thigh, and Leister, with a scream of rage and pain, slashed with his dagger at his friend's sword hand, gashing him viciously. Ignoring the blood, they went back to their deadly work.

By now their battle cries and clashing swords had awakened the colony, and several men came racing down the beach, led by Miles Standish. The captain was furious. With Indians all around them, no one had a right to risk his life, much less commit murder. Disarming the two culprits at the point of his own rapier, Standish marched them shamefacedly back to Governor William Bradford, who was as angry as the captain.

Sitting as judge, Bradford gave the two young men a stern lecture, and then as punishment ordered them strung up with head and heels tied together to "cool off their hot blood." They were also condemned to twenty-four hours of fasting. But within an hour their cries for mercy became so pitiful that Stephen Hopkins went to Bradford and asked him to pardon them, promising that he guaranteed their good behavior. Bradford was happy to agree and quickly ordered them cut down. Ironically, neither Dotey nor Leister ever married the fair Constance. Perhaps impressed by the dangers of idle flirting, she waited another seven years, and then chose a newcomer from England.

Meanwhile the new governor was grappling with far more serious problems. Massasoit's braves and their families continued to arrive in town in annoying numbers, and Bradford decided it was time to make some adjustments in their Indian relations. He therefore appointed Edward Winslow, their fledgling diplomat, and Stephen Hopkins, their man of experience in the New World, as envoys and ordered them to visit the great chief in his village.

Bradford also felt that it was time to do a little more exploring. He was not entirely prepared to take Squanto's word for everything about the Indians surrounding them. He also wanted to know the quickest route to Sowams, should they need to call on Massasoit for armed support. Finally, he was anxious to make peace with any other tribes in the vicinity, particularly the aggressive Nausets who had attacked them so ferociously on Cape Cod.

Squanto agreed to accompany the envoys as guide and interpreter. Bradford provided them with a cloak of red cotton, fringed with lace, as a gift for their noble ally, plus some smaller presents. On Sunday, July 1, the whole colony joined in solemn prayer for the safety and success of the mission. It was no small task that these two men were undertaking, to travel alone through unexplored country, never certain that they might not meet hostile Indians, with nothing to protect them but Squanto's tongue and their uncertain muskets.

They set out on July 2 at 9 o'clock and tramped all day to reach a village called Namasket, near present-day Middleboro. It was from here that many of the visitors to Plymouth came, and the Englishmen were considerably surprised to discover that it was fifteen miles away. The citizens of Namasket received them in a most friendly manner, giving them corn bread and the "spawn of shads" which the white men found delicious when cooked with acorns. They then put on a brief exhibition of marksmanship for their Indian friends. Seeing a crow in the cornfield, one of the Indians asked the white men to kill it. Hopkins, an experienced shot, picked off the bird at eighty yards, which left the Indians gasping with astonishment.

The envoys then continued their journey, passing many Indians fishing in the Titicut River and noticing with amazement the extensively cleared fields. Squanto explained that thousands had lived in this region but that the great plague of four years before had cut them down. Early Tuesday morning they met six of Massasoit's braves, who decided to accompany them. They soon reached the bank of the Taunton River, and the Indians led them to a ford where they began to wade across. In the midst of this operation they suddenly heard a menacing shout from the high grass on the other side of the river. Two Indians, one close to seventy, rose up with drawn bows. They were the remnant of a once numerous village, but they were still prepared to defend their homesite with all their traditional courage and ferocity.

The Indians who were with Winslow and Hopkins quickly reassured them, and the two men were soon offering friendship and food. Leaving a few trinkets with these guardians of the ford, the envoys marched on. A little later one of their Indians spotted someone moving through the forest and quickly warned the rest. Everyone was instantly alert, and the two white men asked why they were so nervous. The Indians explained that they feared even a single Narragansett.

They pushed on, meeting several Indians along the way, all of whom generously shared what food they had with them. If they had any doubt about Massasoit's promise of peace and friendship, it vanished by the time they reached the great chief's village. There they found that Massasoit was off on a visit of his own, and they had to wait until Wednesday, July 4, for his arrival. They greeted him by firing off their muskets and then delivered their gifts to him.

Winslow coolly pointed out that the gifts were not given out of fear but because Plymouth desired continued peace, especially with them, their nearest neighbors. The young envoy then took up the delicate topic of the Wampanoags overfrequent visiting in Plymouth. He pointed out that most of the braves brought wives and children with them and since they were the great chief's subjects, the colonists were anxious to entertain them well, but they were running short of supplies and had no idea what kind of corn harvest they might have. They therefore asked the chief to put a stop to this indiscriminate visiting.

On the other hand if the chief himself wished to come or wished to send any special friend, Governor Bradford had sent him a copper chain which the chief might give to his envoy. Anyone wearing this chain would be welcomed and entertained as if he were the chief himself. Finally Winslow asked Massasoit if he would undertake diplomacy on their behalf with the Indians on Cape Cod. Winslow explained how they had taken corn from these people during the first voyages of discovery and that they now wished to pay for this corn either in kind from their own harvest or in trade.

Massasoit now put on the red cloak and copper chain. "He was not a little proud to behold himself and his men also to see their King so bravely attired," Winslow says. The chief then told the envoys that they were welcome and that he would gladly continue peace and friendship between the two peoples. As for his men, they would pester Plymouth no more. He would also send envoys to the Pamet Indians on Cape Cod, who were the owners of the corn.

The chief then turned to his men and made a great speech. Was not he, Massasoit, commander of the country about them? Was not such and such a town his and the people of it? Would they not bring their skins to trade with the white men in Plymouth? Each time, his braves answered that they were his and that they would be at peace with Plymouth and bring their beaver skins to the settlers. The first few times that this performance was repeated the envoys were delighted, but unfortunately the great chief enumerated at least thirty different towns and grew somewhat tedious.

The speech finally over, the envoys smoked a pipe with the chief and talked at length of England and King James. Massasoit seemed most amazed to discover that the king was a widower (Queen Anne had died in 1619) and had never remarried. The talk went on until darkness fell and the envoys began to feel the pangs of hunger. They looked around for dinner and saw none forthcoming. Finally Massasoit explained that having just come home, he did not have a scrap of food in the house.

Concealing their dismay, the envoys said they were weary and ready for sleep. Whereupon the chief insisted that they share the royal couch with himself and his wife. It was hardly a downy bed of ease. Winslow describes it as "planks laid a foot from the ground and a mat upon them." Later in the night two of the chief's braves wandered in and joined the group, practically squashing the white men. There was also the problem of lice and fleas with which the great chief's wigwam abounded—and the Indian habit of singing themselves to sleep. "We were worse weary of our lodging," Winslow says, "than of our journey."

The next day, many sachems and minor chiefs from surrounding villages poured in to see the white men. The Indians entertained with wrestling matches and races. Winslow and Hopkins challenged them to a shooting contest for beaver skins, but the red men declined. One of them, however, set up a mark on a distant tree and dared them to hit it. This time Hopkins decided to exhibit another kind of weapon and filled his gun with bird shot. The Indians were amazed to see the mark so full of holes.

Noon passed and one o'clock, and still there was no sign

of food. Then Massasoit appeared with two good-sized bass which he had caught in the nearby river. They were promptly thrown into the pot for boiling, and the white men retired to the chief's wigwam, anticipating a feast. To their dismay, they discovered that no less than forty of the tribe crowded around for a share of the two fish.

The envoys were now close to collapse from lack of sleep and food. Before they went to bed they informed Massasoit that they were leaving in the morning. The chief was aware that he had not entertained them particularly well and begged them to stay longer. But when they explained that they wished to spend their Sabbath at Plymouth, he let them go, sending with them one Hobomok, a *pinese,* or warrior of special courage and wisdom, who was to remain at Plymouth for many years as Massasoit's ambassador in residence.

Winslow and Hopkins were so busy with their diplomacy, they were unable to learn much about their Indian friends' less obvious customs, such as their religion. They came away from this visit with the impression that they had none. But on subsequent embassies to the great chief, Winslow was to correct this error, and a few years later write a most respectful and interesting little treatise on the beliefs of his neighbors, for the enlightenment of friends in England.

"They conceive of many Divine Powers," he wrote. "So of one, whom they called Kiehtan, to be the principal and maker of all the rest; and to be made by none. 'He,' say they, 'created the heavens, earth, sea and all creatures contained therein.' Also that he made one man and one woman; of whom they and we and all mankind came: but how they became so far dispersed, that know they not.

"At first, they say, there was no sachem or king but Kieh-tan; who dwells above in the heavens; whither all good men go when they die, to see their friends and have their fill of all things. . . . His habitation lies far westward in the heavens, they say.

"Thither bad men go also, and knock at his door, but he bids them *Quatchet,* that is to say 'walk abroad! for there is no place for such.' So that they wander in restless want and penury. . . ."

Winslow went on to describe other interesting aspects of Indian beliefs. Along with Kiehtan, they worshipped another Power, Hobbamock, who resembled the Christian idea of the Devil. This God supposedly had power over natural creatures, including the ability to heal human sickness. Whenever a warrior was wounded or ill, he would call upon Hobbamock, and he often appeared to them in the shape of a man, a deer, a fawn, an eagle—but most often as a snake.

The *Powah* or tribal medicine man was thought to have special skill in calling upon the devil to heal disease. A *pinese* was also believed to have a special covenant with Hobbamock to preserve him from death by wounds with arrows or knives. Partly because of this belief, and partly because of their superior strength and fighting ability, a single *pinese* had been known to rout a hundred men in a battle.

On the return journey young Winslow had a chance to demonstrate that firmness was as much a part of diplomacy as courteous words. Six braves accompanied them, and while the people along the way proved to be as friendly as before, offering them food and tobacco wherever they stopped, one of their escorts was a surly fellow who made no attempt to help the white men as they crossed various streams or made their camp for the night. At one point he wandered away and came back boasting of some tobacco he had stolen from one of their hosts.

In the village of Namasket, the last stop before Plymouth, Winslow and Hopkins gave gifts to the other Indians who had "showed us any kindness." The surly fellow promptly complained and began listing all the things he had done for the white men. Winslow countered by enumerating the "discourtesies offered us." They told the brave he deserved nothing and then gave him a trinket. The Indian then offered the white men some of his stolen tobacco. Winslow and Hopkins curtly refused it.

Bluntly, before the whole village, they told the fellow that the "men of Plymouth would not receive that which was stolen upon any terms." The citizens of Namasket were greatly impressed, and a little later the same Indian showed how thoroughly cowed he was by offering to carry Winslow across a river. The young envoy accepted, and, after marching the last few miles in a drenching rainstorm, he and Hopkins arrived at Plymouth, wet and weary but far more certain of their ability to deal with their Indian friends and foes.

Chapter 15

War or peace?

Toward the end of July the Billingtons became a public problem once more. Sixteen-year-old John, the brother of the lad who had almost blown up the *Mayflower*, vanished into the woods. The colonists searched in vain for him and finally sent a message to Massasoit asking if he had any news of the boy. The great chief sent runners to the surrounding villages, and they returned with word that young Billington was safe after a rather remarkable journey. He had spent five days in the woods living on berries and had wandered twenty miles out on Cape Cod to the village of Manomet. The Indians there, for some unexplained reason, had taken him farther out on the Cape and had left him with the hostile Nausets. But they had done no harm to him and were perfectly willing to surrender him if the white men would kindly come and collect him.

Governor Bradford promptly decided that this was an excellent opportunity to make peace with the Nausets. He chose ten armed men, and late in July they set out in the shallop for a return cruise up the coast of Cape Cod. Both Squanto and Hobomok came along as interpreters. The day they sailed was hot and sunny, but they were at sea only a few hours when their little shallop was engulfed in a wild summer storm. Thunder and lightning raged around them, and what looked like a water spout rose not far away. But they rode out the blast and at nightfall anchored in Cummaquid (present-day Barnstable) harbor.

In the morning they found the tide out and their boat high and dry. Not far away, in the channel, were several Indians hunting lobsters. Bradford sent his two interpreters to ask the whereabouts of young Billington, and they replied that the boy was well but was farther down the coast at the village of Aspinet, chief of the Nausets.

The lobster fishermen graciously invited the white men to come ashore and eat with them. Taking no chances, Bradford insisted that four of them must stay as hostages in the boat while he and six of his amateur troopers went ashore. It was an unnecessary precaution. The sachem, or local chief, a young man named Iyanough, was a gracious host and an entirely delightful person. Bradford describes him as "gentle, courteous and fair conditioned: indeed not like a savage save for his attire. His entertainment was answerable to his parts and his cheer plentiful and various."

They sat down to an excellent lunch of broiled lobster and fish, followed by Indian dancing and singing, which Iyanough obviously relished. Only one thing marred the otherwise pleasant visit. A ragged Indian woman who looked to Bradford no less than a hundred years old hobbled up to the feasting visitors and began to weep and moan and tear her hair. Somberly Iyanough explained that she had never seen an Englishman before but that she could not behold them without weeping because she was the mother of three sons whom the treacherous Captain Hunt had kidnapped into slavery with Squanto.

It was a tense moment. Bradford rose to the occasion. In the name of all Englishmen, he apologized for the existence of Captain Hunt. He was a bad man, and every Englishman who heard of it condemned him for such a vicious act. The men of Plymouth would never injure their Indian friends in this way, even though it gained them all the beaver skins in the country. They then gave the weeping old woman some bright trinkets which seemed to lessen her grief somewhat.

Iyanough generously offered to accompany Bradford and serve as an additional proof of friendship for the suspicious Nausets. The chief and two of his braves therefore boarded the shallop, and they set out down the coast once more. When they reached Nauset (present-day Eastham) night was falling, and a low tide prevented them from getting close to shore. However, Iyanough and his men waded to land, and Squanto went with them to inform the Nausets of Governor Bradford's presence.

Soon the beach was crowded with dozens of Nauset warriors and their wives and children. They made signs for the white men to come closer, but the tide prevented them. Bradford had no desire to do so anyway—this tribe had attacked them once before, and he was not going to give them another chance. The men in the boat were amazed by the number of Indians on the beach. How did their exploring parties wander up and down the shore for so many weeks without seeing a single one of them?

Finally, the tide permitted the boat to come closer. The Indians crowded around, but Bradford placed an armed guard on the prow and let only two men into the boat. One of these was a Pamet, from the village from which the corn had been taken. Once more Bradford explained why they had taken it and offered him complete restitution if he would come to Plymouth to collect it. The man promised to come, and they gave him some small presents.

Not long after sunset, the Nauset chief Aspinet appeared with no less than a hundred armed braves around him. Walking beside him, no doubt grinning with delight, was John Billington, Jr., covered from head to foot with brightly colored beads. Aspinet and fifty of his men laid down their bows and arrows and walked out to the shallop with the boy. The other fifty stood within firing range with their bows and arrows ready. The Nausets did not trust the white men any more than the white men trusted them. But there were no hostilities on either side. Aspinet handed over young Billington, and Bradford rewarded him with a fine English knife. He gave another knife to the Indian who had first found the boy and brought him to Aspinet. The governor and the sachem exchanged promises of peace, and the Indians withdrew.

Squanto then told Bradford some very disquieting news. According to Aspinet, the powerful Narragansetts who had been untouched by the plague that had weakened all the other tribes had launched war on Massasoit. They had reportedly killed a number of his men and had captured the chief himself. Plymouth might well be in danger. Bradford reacted with alarm. There were only twenty-two adult males left in Plymouth. He had taken the ten best men with him in the shallop.

They immediately set sail for home, but the wind proved uncooperative, and they were forced to land once more. Their fresh water was low, and they began searching for a pond or brook to replenish their barrels. Fumbling along in the dark, they met Iyanough with a great crowd of men and women from his village who had gone down the beach to meet their chief on the way home. While the good-natured sachem led the water party to a nearby runlet, the Indian women joined hands and sang and danced around the shallop.

Unfortunately, the water they brought back was brackish, but in the morning they invited the young chief on board the boat and sailed down to Cummaquid, his native village, where they found fresh water and more friendly feasting and entertainment from this personable and pleasant red man.

They pushed on quickly to Plymouth, however, and there they found everyone safe but deeply disturbed by more rumors of war. They, too, had heard reports that the Narragansetts had captured Massasoit and taken over the surrounding country. Quickly the worried Bradford sent Squanto and Hobomok out to the neighboring villages to find out what was happening.

For the next few days the men of Plymouth prepared to defend themselves. The thirty-two able-bodied men were drilled and lectured by Miles Standish, and gun crews were rehearsed in the art of loading and firing the cannon on Fort Hill. Then Hobomok came racing into town with most alarming news. The upheaval begun by rumors of the Narragansetts' hostilities had spread almost to Plymouth's gates.

Massasoit was in the hands of the Narragansetts, though it would be stretching it a bit to call him a prisoner. He had apparently gone as a suppliant, endeavoring to continue the precarious truce between them and his own tribe. Meanwhile at Namasket, the sachem Corbitant, supposedly loyal to Massasoit but long suspected of being too friendly with the Narragansetts, decided to alter the balance of power. He began making speeches to the braves of his village, denouncing Massasoit's peaceful policy with Plymouth and sneering at the recent treaties of peace which the white men had negotiated between the Nausets and Iyanough's tribe.

Corbitant's rage soon focused on Squanto, whom he accused of being the chief architect of this treacherous policy of peace. Squanto and Hobomok were staying at Namasket, hoping to learn more about the fate of Massasoit. Suddenly they found guards around their house and Corbitant announcing that he intended to kill them both. He then dragged Squanto out of the house, shouting that if he were dead the English would "lose their tongue." When Corbitant began brandishing a knife at Hobomok's throat, the pinese had fought his way past the guards and had raced to Plymouth with the bad news that Squanto was probably dead.

Governor Bradford immediately summoned his council to an emergency session. Once more the new leaders of Plymouth were faced with a crucial policy decision. How should

they react to these insults offered their friends and envoys?
Should they strive for a peaceful solution or should they answer insult with insult, force with force? They were men of
peace. They wanted peace. But they wisely recognized that
sometimes the best way to achieve it is through strength.

On Tuesday, August 14, ten men under the command of
Miles Standish set out for Namasket. It rained all the way,
but they did not let the weather distract or delay them. Four
miles from the village, they halted in the woods, waiting for
night to fall. Standish decided to attack at midnight, surrounding Corbitant's house and hopefully rescuing Squanto
if he was still alive. If he was dead, the captain grimly announced he was going to kill Corbitant in revenge.

It continued to rain. In the darkness and wet, even Hobomok became confused and lost his way, but Stephen Hopkins,
who had made the trip before, showed himself a superior
woodsman by bringing them to the edge of the village. All
was quiet. They sat down, and Standish ordered them to eat
supper from their knapsacks—men fought better with food
in their stomachs.

They then moved stealthily into the sleeping village and
surrounded Corbitant's hut. Drawing their swords, Standish
and two other men charged inside. In a voice of thunder, the
captain ordered no one to move—anyone who tried to escape
would be instantly killed; only the women and children had
nothing to fear.

Chaos erupted. The screams of the women mingled with
the frightened roars of the braves. Three Indians tried to
break out through a secret door and were wounded by the
swords of those surrounding the hut. Inside, frightened

women clung to Hobomok, calling him "friend," and many boys, thinking that they were going to be murdered, were screaming "I am a girl." But Squanto was not in the hut, nor was Corbitant. Where were they?

By now the whole village was awake. Standish ordered two muskets to be fired into the air to discourage anyone who might be inclined to attack them. Hobomok, meanwhile, got up on top of the hut and began calling for Squanto. In a few minutes, up strode Plymouth's best friend, not dead, not even wounded. There were a number of braves with him whom Standish promptly disarmed, promising to return their bows and arrows at daylight. The white men then explained why they had come in such warlike fashion and learned that in the uproar Corbitant and his faction had fled.

Standish and his men stayed in the village all night, and in the morning most of the Indians came and greeted them in a warm and friendly manner. Standish then made a grim speech. Although Corbitant had escaped for the moment, he said, there was no place in the land where he would be safe if he continued to threaten Plymouth and mock Massasoit's great treaty of peace. Corbitant had come to Plymouth more than once and had been kindly entertained there. They had never showed nor intended any evil toward him, nor did they now if he was willing to make peace with them. As for the great chief Massasoit, if he did not return in safety from the Narragansetts, Plymouth would make war on them and overthrow them.

It was a daring speech for a man with only thirty-two soldiers, but Standish was a shrewd judge of human nature. He knew that the crucial factor in the relations between two peoples was power and that the Indians were still deeply afraid of his muskets. For Plymouth's salvation, he was determined to press the advantage as long as it lasted. Never, while Miles Standish was alive, did this new commonwealth react to insult with weakness.

Perhaps the highest compliment Standish earned for his exploit was the lifelong admiration of Hobomok, something not easily won from a pinese. It was the beginning of a deep friendship between the white warrior and the red warrior. In his extreme old age when Hobomok became quite feeble, Standish took him into his home and cared for him until his death.

Now, as proof of their peaceful intentions, Standish offered to take anyone who had been wounded in the first melee back to Plymouth, where Doctor Samuel Fuller would heal them. One man and a woman accepted his invitation, and accompanied by Squanto and "many other known friends" the ten soldiers and their warrior captain marched home with peace restored.

Chapter 16

THANKSGIVING DAY

Within a few days after the expedition to Namas-ket, the wisdom of Plymouth's policy of strength became apparent. Congratulations and promises of peace from sachems as far away as Martha's Vineyard poured into the little settlement. Massasoit returned unharmed from the Narragansetts, and a humbled Corbitant went to the great chief and asked him if he would help the rabble-rouser make peace with Plymouth.

Now the energy and decision of Plymouth's new leaders manifested itself in another exploration. For some time they had been hearing news of the Massachusetts Indians who lived around the shores of a great bay twenty leagues to the north. They were a warlike people, and many of the messages that Plymouth had heard were filled with threats and scorn. The sensible thing to do, William Bradford decided, was to send envoys to them to see the country, make peace with them, and see what they had to trade.

Once more the governor chose ten men, this time under Miles Standish, and sent Squanto and two other Indians along in the shallop. They set out at midnight on September 18 and reached Boston Harbor late the following day. They went ashore the next morning and breakfasted on delicious lobsters that had been gathered by Indian fishermen. Then Captain Standish briskly set two sentinels on a cliff to secure the shallop and marched inland with a squad of four.

They met a woman who said she had caught the lobsters that they had eaten, so they gave her some trinkets which more than satisfied her. Soon, with the woman's help, they reached the village of a local sachem named Obbatinewat. He was an ally of Massasoit and greeted them in a most friendly fashion. He had little to offer them in the way of hospitality, however. He lived a rather miserable life, continuously in fear of the fierce Abnaki Indians of Maine, who raided his people constantly. The squaw sachem, or queen of the Massachusetts, was also one of his enemies.

Captain Standish told Obbatinewat of all the sachems who had come to Plymouth after their show of force at Namasket and had allied themselves with King James. If Obbatinewat wished to join this alliance, Standish grandly guaranteed to safeguard him from his enemies. The sachem eagerly agreed and offered to lead them across the bay to the residence of the Massachusetts squaw queen.

Landing near present-day Charlestown, Standish marched all but two of his men three miles inland. Here they came to a place where corn had just been harvested and where a wigwam had been pulled down in great haste. Obviously, news of the white men's arrival had spread through the countryside, and the immediate reaction was fear.

In another mile they came to the house of the late king of the Massachusetts, Nanepashemet. It was an unusual structure, completely unlike any Indian dwelling they had seen. Standing high upon a hill, the house was built on a huge scaffold some six feet from the ground. Not far away was a fort that the king had built. A wall of great trees some thirty or forty feet high was dug into the ground, enclosing a ring of some forty or fifty square feet. A trench, breast high, was dug on either side of it, and the only entrance was over a small bridge. In the center of this strange structure was a wigwam in which the great chief lay buried.

Standish now decided they had gone far enough from their shallop and sent two of his Indians on ahead to look for the inhabitants. The envoys soon returned with good news. The Massachusetts braves had apparently fled into the forest, but the women were nearby guarding the corn. The explorers marched another mile to reach them, seeing more evidence en route of houses hastily pulled down and corn covered only by a single mat.

The squaws trembled with fear as the white men approached, but they soon saw that no harm was meant and fell to boiling cod and other food, entertaining them in excellent style. Finally one of their men came out of the forest, shaking and trembling as much as the women. He was relieved to find that no hostilities were intended and was more than willing to trade his beaver skins with Plymouth. All the Indian women were well dressed in coats of luxurious beaver, and Squanto, betraying his primitive heritage, suggested to Standish that they rob their coats and corn and everything else that might be useful. "They are a bad people," he said, "and have often threatened you."

Proving he was no warmonger, Standish replied: "Were they never so bad, we would not wrong them or give them any justification against us." He went on to explain to the puzzled Squanto that the white men put little stock in the harsh words that the Massachusetts flung about, but let them do something against Plymouth and then "we would deal far worse than he desired."

The Massachusetts women accompanied the explorers back to their shallop and were so eager to trade that they sold the beaver coats from their backs and tied boughs about themselves to protect their modesty. "But with great shame-facedness," Edward Winslow says, and thinking of the low-cut gowns he had seen on London jezebels, he adds, "for indeed they are more modest than some of our English women."

Standish and his men were awed on the way home by the magnificence of Massachusetts Bay. "Better harbors for shipping cannot be than here are," Edward Winslow said. Sailing home with a good load of beaver, the Plymouth men wondered aloud if they had chosen the wrong site for their homestead. When they mentioned their doubts to William Bradford, the young governor vehemently disagreed. It would be folly to abandon Plymouth. They had invested too much in labor and Indian diplomacy. The *Mayflower* had carried their application for a patent on this land. "The Lord assigns to all men the bounds of their habitation," he said. Massachusetts Bay must have been appointed for another use.

Besides, Governor Bradford pointed out, they had much to be thankful for. They had twenty acres of corn almost ready to harvest and a firm friendship with the Indians in their vicinity. The woods and rivers teemed with game and fish. They were no longer threatened by either starvation or annihilation. Instead of wondering about the advantages of Massachusetts Bay, perhaps they should all offer thanks to God for the blessings he had given them here at Plymouth.

As the son of an English farmer, William Bradford was well acquainted with the harvest celebrations of his homeland. He also remembered the annual Thanksgiving Day celebrated in Leyden on the third of October, the anniversary of the city's deliverance from the Spaniards. Why not have a similar holiday here in Plymouth so that they might "after a more special manner rejoice together"?

Preparations for the first Thanksgiving Day were soon under way. The twenty acres of Indian corn yielded an excellent harvest, but the six acres of English barley and peas came to nothing. This emphasized in everyone's mind how deeply dependent they were on their Indian allies. Without the corn they would face a winter of certain starvation. No doubt this was a major reason why Governor Bradford decided that their Indian friends should also come to the festival.

A messenger was sent to Massasoit inviting him. Governor Bradford then sent four men out fowling, and in one day they killed enough wild turkeys to feed the whole company for almost a week. There were also eels, lobsters, and shellfish gathered from the bountiful shores of the bay. But not even this abundance seemed enough when the great Chief Massasoit arrived with no less than ninety hungry men.

For a moment, even that budding diplomat Edward Winslow was speechless. Ninety braves! Knowing by now the Indian tendency to gorge as long as food was available, the colonists saw all their provisions for the winter vanishing. They did not realize that for Massasoit and his Wampanoags a harvest thanksgiving was also a customary festival. Almost all the tribes along the eastern seaboard celebrated the ripening of the crops with a "Green Corn Dance." Among many, this feast lasted for days, during which the entire village was cleansed and renewed, all old clothes and provisions discarded, and new fires kindled, to symbolize the beginning of a new year.

Massasoit and his men assumed they were being invited to Plymouth's version of this feast and thus knew what was expected of them. They promptly sent hunters into the woods, who came back with five "fine deer." These they presented ceremoniously to the leaders of the little colony— Governor Bradford, Miles Standish, Edward Winslow, William Brewster, Stephen Hopkins. The venison was accepted with gratitude. Nor was this the end of the Indians' generosity. Almost certainly they exhibited their skill in catching eels and other sea creatures, to further bulwark the common larder.

The menu on this first thanksgiving was by no means confined to meat and fish. The household gardens had produced a great variety of vegetables—"sallets," as the citizens of 1621 called them: parsnips, carrots, turnips, onions, cu-

cumbers, radishes, beets, cabbages. The wild fruits of the summer—gooseberries, strawberries, plums, and cherries—had been dried under Squanto's expert instructions, and some were cooked in "dough cases" to become forerunners of New England's famous pies. Although the nearby bogs abounded in cranberries, their first use had to wait some years—and then it was in a "steamed pudding" made from chopped cranberries, flour, and molasses. The Indians also grew pumpkins among their corn—and Squanto undoubtedly obtained some seeds for the colonists—but in this first year there is no evidence that this formidable vegetable found its way onto Plymouth's tables. In later years, however, the colonists would be eating pumpkin regularly as sauce and in bread and in pie.

One joy to the palate which they did have in abundance was wine. Since their beer had run short, they wasted no time in brewing both white and red from the wild grapes that grew "very sweet and strong" throughout the countryside. The vintage must have been a trifle green that first October, and they may have spiked it with Holland gin or other "strong waters" which they had in plenty among their stores. For Massasoit and his braves, this first taste of the transformed juice of the grape was further proof of the magic powers of their new allies.

For biscuits and bread there was English wheat, which they used sparingly, since their supply was very limited. But corn they had in abundance, and they served it parched and in hoecakes and in ashcakes. It tasted even better roasted over the hot coals and dipped in butter. Squanto added a local dish, Indian pudding, made of cornmeal and molasses boiled in a bag. It is also highly probable that everyone enjoyed this "grain that built a continent" in another New World way—cooked over the coals in earthen jars until the kernels burst into fluffy whiteness—popcorn! The Indians had been eating it this way for decades, and they also knew how to add the final touch by pouring maple syrup over it to turn it into sweet crunchy balls of goo.

The cooking was almost all done in the open—the venison and turkeys and geese and partridges turned on spits, the lobsters and oysters roasted over the coals, the clam chowder and venison stews simmered in iron kettles over dancing fires. There were only ten women, counting teen-agers, to do the cooking. But the men turned the spits and sliced the venison and generally helped with the heavy work.

Between meals, the guests and hosts relaxed in games of sport and skill. There were shooting exhibitions with both guns and bows. Massasoit and his men were impressed to discover that some of these white men, especially Miles Standish, could handle a bow and arrow almost as well as an Indian. The red men were delighted to find that John Alden, John Howland, and the other younger men were ready and eager to join them in their races and wrestling matches. In return Plymouth's athletes introduced them to their favorite sport, stoolball, which involved batting a ball through a series of wickets in a sort of rough-and-tumble croquet.

Captain Standish entertained with military maneuvers. Choosing his best men, he marched the company briskly down the main street into the clearing where the feast was being held.

"Rest your muskets," he barked. The men expertly thrust their pieces in the spikelike rest that supported the heavy matchlock from the ground during firing.

"Draw out your match." The long match was made ready. "Try your match. Guard your pan. Present. Give fire!"

The volley boomed out, to the Indians' mixture of delight and dismay.

"Bring up your musket," the captain shouted. "Poise your musket and recover your rest. Shoulder your musket."

Always quick to seize an opportunity to impress his Indian allies, Standish climaxed his military parade by firing one of the cannons on Fort Hill. With the same brisk military order, the big gun was loaded (but not shotted) and the match was applied to the touchhole by the captain himself. Whoom! The Indians had been astounded by the crash of the white men's muskets. But this mighty gun seemed to steal the thunder from heaven itself. Truly Massasoit had been wise to make peace with these people! Perhaps they could overthrow even the mighty Narragansetts if they chose.

But display of power was not the main purpose of this feast; by far the largest part of it was devoted to uninhibited drinking and eating and gaiety. Proof of how well Governor Bradford succeeded as master of ceremonies is in the duration of the celebration—three long full days of marathon enjoyment. During the nights, Massasoit and his braves slept in the fields around Plymouth. Gone were the fears that once made a worried Standish post extra guards against a treacherous attack. By the time this first Thanksgiving was over, the formal alliance between Plymouth and the men of Massasoit had been cemented by strong ties of genuine friendship. Red men and white men parted, vowing to repeat the feast the following year and for many years to come.

Chapter 17

HELP FROM HOME

The great feast over, Plymouth settled down to a
more somber routine. Winter was not far away now. The
trees were a riot of russet and gold and the air had an
ominous autumn chill. But they were reasonably well prepared. From their corn supply, they were able to guarantee
about a peck a week to each person as well as another peck
of the meal that they had brought from England. They took
advantage of the southward migration of ducks and other
wild fowl to lay in a good supply of them, as well as venison,
against the lean winter months.

Besides hunting, there was much to be done on the houses,
adding thatch to roofs, daubing chinks with clay. All this
work was suddenly interrupted by an excited Indian who
came racing into town with news from Cape Cod. There was
a ship sailing toward Plymouth. A great ship with sails. A
white man's ship!

Everyone stared, at first with amazement then with concern. They expected no ship from England. Who could it be? Their first thought was a French or Spanish privateer, for the land on which they stood was claimed by both these traditional enemies of England. Quickly Bradford called his council together and ordered the cannon on the hill to be fired as an alarm to those who were out hunting or fishing.

Miles Standish now took over, stationing small squads of men along the shore to repel landing parties and priming his artillery on Fort Hill. If it was an enemy, they were going to fight. Not for them the habit of buying off marauding pirates and privateers as so many Spanish cities did farther south.

Hours of waiting passed, and then the mysterious visitor was visible off the entrance to the harbor. He was coming in! Breathlessly they watched the captain feeling his way down the channel with the leadsman heaving away in the bowsprit. Soon he was past Saquish Head and swinging about to anchor near Clark's Island, not far from where the *Mayflower* had ridden. Now was the moment. If he was a privateer, a foreign flag would run up his masthead.

But no, there riding up the mast was the red and white cross of St. George. They were English! Briskly the newcomers lowered away boats and rowed for shore. The citizens of Plymouth crowded down to the beach to welcome them. Who was that standing up in the prow of the lead boat? Could it be—yes, their old friend Robert Cushman! It was help from home, not a stray fisherman in search of fresh water or a curious trader on the way to Virginia, but their friends who had not forgotten them.

For William Brewster there was special joy. His twenty-eight-year-old son Jonathan stepped ashore. Edward Winslow joyfully embraced his brothers, John and Kenelm. All together there were thirty-five passengers on board the good ship *Fortune,* most of them men and all healthy. They had had only one death on the way over, a man named Ford whose widow, Martha, gave birth to a son the night she landed. Within eighteen months she would be married to Peter Brown.

Among the new men were some welcome skills. William Wright was an expert carpenter, and Stephen Dean was an experienced miller, who eventually built a small mill to grind the colony's corn. Robert Hicks's wife was later to become the town's first schoolteacher. Philipe de la Noye, a young French Huguenot, was not especially distinguished and never became a leader at Plymouth, but in centuries to come he would acquire some posthumous fame as the first American ancestor of Franklin Delano Roosevelt.

Plymouth was delighted to see its thin ranks filled by these new recruits, although William Bradford was somewhat disturbed to discover that they had brought not so much as a "biscuit cake" in provisions, nor had they bedding or any other household goods with them. It meant the colony would have to go on short rations for the winter. But this was a minor problem compared to the enormous significance of these new arrivals in other ways.

Robert Cushman had with him a new patent from the Council for New England confirming their possession of Plymouth and their shipboard compact and authorizing them to establish laws and ordinances for governing themselves on a majority-rule basis. Cushman's collapse and withdrawal at the beginning of the voyage now seemed a providential thing. His presence in England had played a vital part in getting prompt approval of their patent, and he had also smoothed over the quarrel with their merchant backers and had persuaded them to send the *Fortune* with these badly needed reinforcements. Cushman returned to London with the *Fortune* and until his death in 1625 was to do extremely effective work as their representative, continuing, in Bradford's admiring words, "to be a special instrument for their good and to do the offices of a loving friend and faithful brother unto them."

The new colonists were well pleased with what they found in "New Plymouth." The *Fortune* carried back with it to England a letter from one of the arrivals, a young man named William Hilton, who summed up their impressions.

Loving Cousin,
At Plymouth in New England we found all our friends and planters in good health, though they were left sick and weak, with very small means. The Indians round about us peaceable and friendly. The country very pleasant and temperate, yielding naturally of itself great store of fruits as vines of diverse and great abundance . . . flocks of turkeys, quails, pigeons and partridges . . . lakes abounding with fish, fowl, beavers and otters. The sea affords us as great plenty, all excellent sorts of sea fish as the rivers and isles doth a variety of wild fowl of most useful sorts. . . . Better grain cannot be than the Indian corn, if planted on as good ground as a man need desire. We are all freeholders, the rent day doth not trouble us and all those good blessings we have of which and what we list in their seasons for taking. Our company are for most part very religious, honest people; the word of God sincerely taught us every Sabbath; so that I know not anything a contented mind can here want. I desire your friendly care to send my wife and children to me where I wish all the friends I have in England.

Plymouth would have more trouble in the years to come. There would be starving times and unnerving litigation over their patent, which was vague about the colony's boundaries, and upsets with the London merchants and with the Indians, although the basic treaty of peace with Massasoit would endure for the lifetime of that good and great chief—another forty years. But as Governor William Bradford looked at the strong bodies and eager faces of the new arrivals, and the ship riding in the harbor, he must have known that the worst was over for him and his fellow exiles. They would survive and prosper.

Others would follow in their footsteps, men of different beliefs, who would found more powerful colonies in Massachusetts Bay, at Hudson's River, and along other great harbors and rivers of this mighty continent. But none would contain the essentials of the American experience, that unique combination of courage and faith, in such pure and dramatic form as little Plymouth. Her story, told by William Bradford in his *History of Plymouth Plantation,* would be the touchstone toward which a great nation would look for values and ideals, in its years of maturity.

Perhaps already William Bradford felt the quiet pride evident in the words he would later write, words that are both the summary and the reason for this book. "As one small candle may light a thousand, so the light kindled here has shown unto many, yea in some sort to our whole nation. . . . We have noted these things so that you might see their worth and not negligently lose what your fathers have obtained with so much hardship."

BIBLIOGRAPHY

Primary Sources

Arber, Edward. *The Story of the Pilgrim Fathers,* edited from the original texts, 1897.

Bradford, William. *Of Plymouth Plantations,* edited by S. E. Morison, 1959.

Young, Alexander. *Chronicles of the Pilgrim Fathers,* 1894.

Secondary Sources

Ames, Aziel. *The Mayflower and Her Log,* 1901.

Archer, Gleason L. *Mayflower Heroes,* 1931.

Linton, Ralph and Adeline. *We Gather Together,* 1949.

Love, W. DeLoss. *Fast and Thanksgiving Days of New England,* 1895.

Mackennal, Alexander. *Homes and Haunts of the Pilgrim Fathers,* 1899.

Marble, Annie Russell. *The Women Who Came in the Mayflower,* 1920.

Morison, Samuel Eliot. *The Story of the Old Colony of New Plymouth,* 1956.

Nickerson, W. Sears. *Land Ho! 1620,* 1931.

Plooij, D. *The Pilgrim Fathers from a Dutch Point of View,* 1932.

Robinson, Charles N. *The British Tar in Fact and Fiction,* 1909.

Smith, Henry Justin. *The Master of the Mayflower,* 1936.

Willison, George F. *Saints and Strangers,* 1945.

INDEX

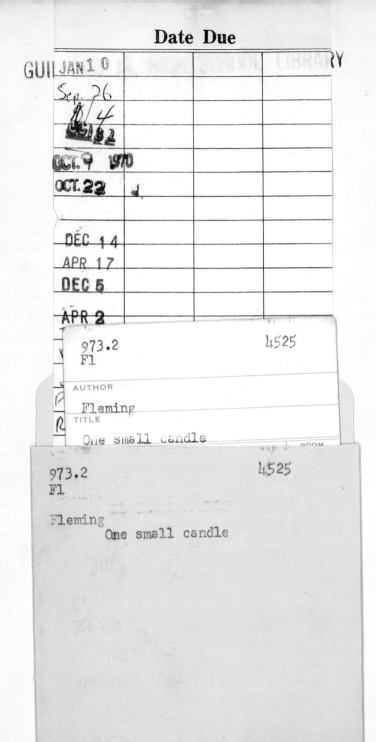